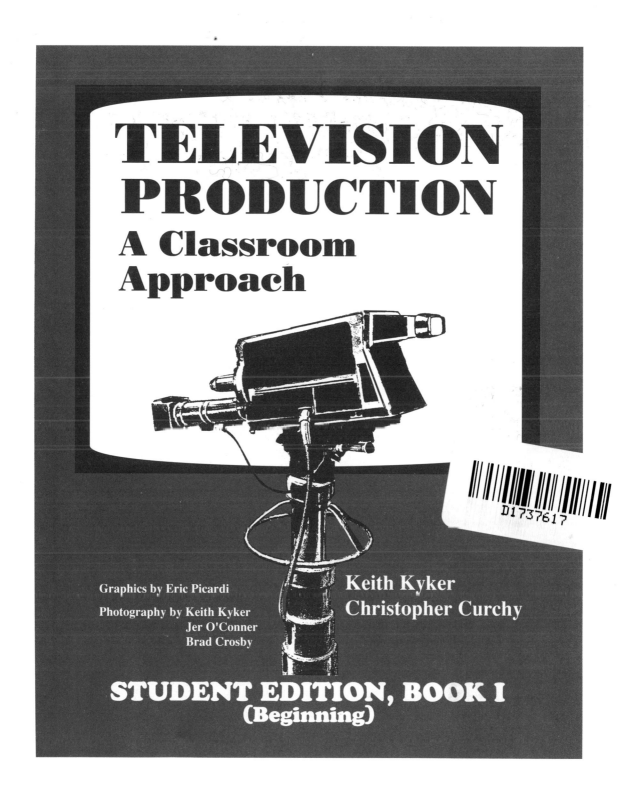

# TELEVISION PRODUCTION
## A Classroom Approach

Graphics by Eric Picardi

Photography by Keith Kyker
Jer O'Conner
Brad Crosby

Keith Kyker
Christopher Curchy

### STUDENT EDITION, BOOK I
(Beginning)

D1737617

1993
LIBRARIES UNLIMITED, INC.
Englewood, Colorado

*To Shelba and Sarah*
—K.K.

*To my family and friends for*
*surrendering their summer.*
—C.C.

LIBRARIES UNLIMITED
P.O. Box 6633
Englewood, CO 80155-6633
1-800-237-6124

**Library of Congress Cataloging-in-Publication Data**

*Suggested cataloging:*

Kyker, Keith.
    Television production : a classroom approach / Keith Kyker and Christopher Curchy. -- Englewood, Colo.: Libraries Unlimited, 1993.
    Includes bibliographical references and index.
    xvi, 378 p.  22x28 cm. (Instructor Edition) ISBN 1-56308-101-6
    iv, 121 p.  22x28 cm. (Student Edition, Book I) ISBN 1-56308-108-3
    iv, 137 p.  22x28 cm. (Student Edition, Book II) ISBN 1-56308-161-X
    27 min. (Video) ISBN 1-56308-107-5
    1. Television production and direction.  2. Television equipment and supplies.  I. Curchy, Christopher.  II. Title.
PN1992.75 K9  1993
791.450232 (DDC 20)

# CONTENTS

# PREFACE

This student textbook is designed to be used as part one of a two-part course in television production. Users should obtain the *Instructor Edition* and the videotape, in addition to the *Student Edition, Book II*, from the publisher to have all of the components for the entire course.

# 1 | BEGINNING TELEVISION PRODUCTION

## Lesson 1 Equipment Orientation

### Objectives

After successfully completing this lesson, you will be able to:

> - name and describe the three main parts of the camera.
> - explain the difference between a camcorder and a camera/deck system.
> - name and describe the two types of imaging devices.
> - explain the need for a tripod in video production.
> - explain the principle and process of audio dubbing.
> - describe the function of the macro lens and name real-world uses for it.
> - operate a camcorder or camera/deck system on a tripod.
> - frame and focus a subject using a macro lens.
> - operate a fade control button.
> - audio-dub over existing audio on a videotape.

### Vocabulary

**Audio dub.** The process of replacing the existing audio track(s) with new audio.

**Camcorder.** A combination video camera and video deck. Camcorders are often less expensive than camera/video deck systems, and are more commonly found in schools.

**Charge-coupled device (CCD).** A photo-sensitive microchip that serves as an imaging device for many video cameras/camcorders manufactured since 1988.

**Imaging device.** The part of a camcorder or video camera that transfers the light that enters the camera into electrical signals.

**Lens.** The curved glass on the front of the camcorder/video camera that selects part of the environment and produces a small image of it onto the imaging device for processing.

**Macro lens.** A separate lens, usually installed within the regular lens, that allows for videography of objects normally too small or too close to the lens to bring into focus.

**Tripod.** A three-legged camera mount used to stabilize camera operation and relieve fatigue.

**Video camera.** A piece of equipment consisting of a lens, viewfinder, imaging device, and internal electronics, that transfers light into electrical signals.

**Video deck.** A device that records the electrical signal generated by the video camera onto magnetic tape. The video deck usually performs playback, rewind, and fast-forward functions. Unlike a home VCR, a video deck does not include a tuner.

**Viewfinder.** A small monitor, usually monochrome (black and white), mounted on top of a video camera or camcorder that allows the camera operator to see the video signal being created by the camera.

Television has often been called "the magic box." When thinking about the amazing technology behind the process of television production, it's easy to see why most viewers think of the medium as magical. As quaint and traditional as this terminology may seem, it brings with it a major problem when teaching the skills of television production. If we see television technology as magical, then we see no way to control, manipulate, or change it. Many students have left television production classes bewildered and confused, not because of a low level of instruction but because they find it impossible to believe that the amazing, magical technology available on their television sets can be mastered by mere mortals.

Therefore, if we are to truly understand the elements of television production, we must stop thinking of the technology as unapproachable. Television production involves a series of machines. These machines perform the tasks for which they are created. To provide a simple analogy, a toaster is a machine that has been created to turn bread into toast. By the same (albeit, much more high-tech) token, a video camera converts light into electrical signals. Both the toaster and the video camera were created to perform certain, useful functions. Each has a series of adjustments that can be made to alter the end product. While most individuals can learn the technique behind making toast in a few minutes, operating television equipment takes longer to master. However, the idea remains the same: Learn what the equipment was designed to do, then learn what you can do to get the most out of the equipment.

## The Camera

The video camera takes in light, and converts that light into an electrical signal. That signal is called video signal. This operation requires three basic elements of the camera: the lens, the viewfinder, and the imaging device (figure 1.1).

The *lens* gathers the light that the camera uses as its raw material. Video camera lenses used by schools usually range from 6 x 1 to 20 x 1. To understand what those numbers mean, we need to understand the concept of focal length. The lens performs according to its focal length—the length from the optical midpoint of the lens to the front of the camera imaging device. A long focal length indicates a powerful lens, one that can magnify and get close-ups of objects far away. A short focal length lens performs in the opposite way. We can get wide-angle shots with a short focal length. A still photographer at a baseball game would probably alternate between two lenses: a long lens, also known as telephoto, to get close-ups of the players on the field, and a short lens, also known as wide-angle, to get shots of the entire field. These are known as fixed focal-length lenses. That's why you

Fig. 1.1. Parts of the video camera.

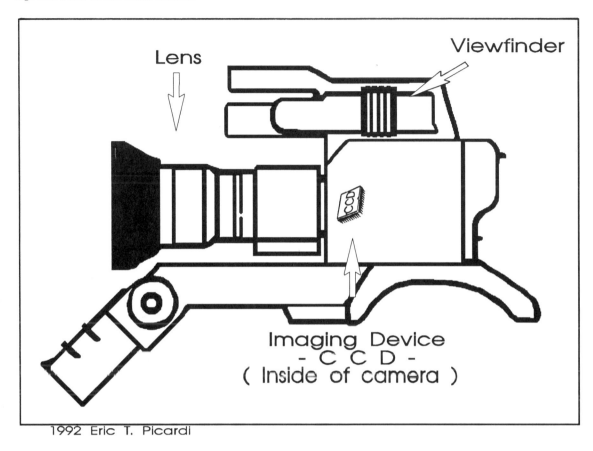

1992 Eric T. Picardi

often see a still photographer with two or more cameras. Its quicker, albeit more expensive, to have two complete cameras than to constantly change lenses.

In order to avoid the multiple-camera/multiple-lens scenario, the *zoom*, or variable focal length lens, was developed. The zoom lens is actually a standard lens that houses another, movable lens inside. By twisting a dial or operating a camera control, a videographer can move that "lens within a lens" to adjust the focal length. Instead of changing the lens on a video camera or camcorder, the videographer simply adjusts his zoom lens.

Now we can get back to the numbers. The zoom lens is described as a ratio. Because many school camcorders have a 12 x 1 zoom lens, let's use that as an example. The second number in the ratio (1, in this case) describes the shortest focal length in millimeters (mm). A focal length of 1 millimeter approximates normal vision. (Remember, a short focal length indicates a wide-angle shot.) The first number (12) indicates the number of times the focal length can be increased. So, in our example, the lens has a *zoom range* of 1mm to 12mm. This lens could capture normal vision in its widest, "zoomed-out" setting and magnify 12 times normal vision. A zoom lens of 50 x 1 would have the same wide angle setting as the 12 x 1 lens, but would be able to "zoom-in" much closer, getting close-up shots at great distances.

Now, let's manipulate the second number. Let's say you've been given a video camera with a 12 x .5 zoom lens. The second number, .5 tells us that this lens will be able to capture wide-angle shots. A photographer could stand reasonably close to a large group and capture each group member in the picture. (School club photographers often use a fixed .5mm lens.) The second number says that the .5 setting can be multiplied 12 times. Twelve x .5mm = 6mm—not very long. Therefore the zoom range of this lens is .5mm to 6mm.

Here's another example. Your lens reads 15 x 8. How can we describe this lens? Looking at the second number, we know that the shortest focal length will be 8mm. This is *not* a wide setting, to say the least. How long can the lens get? 120mm. Wow! You'll be shooting close-ups from across the parking lot!

Don't expect the shape of your zoom lens to visibly change as you change the focal length. Remember, the zoom lens changes *within* the lens housing.

Be careful when using lenses with extremely long (more than 12mm) or extremely short (less than 1mm) focal lengths. The longer, more powerful the lens, the harder it is to steady. You will probably need to use a tripod when videotaping with a long lens. Even the slightest camera movement will shake your subject out of the picture.

Lenses with short focal lengths cause barrel distortion, that strange curving at the right and left sides of the picture. People standing at the extreme sides of the wide-angle shot may appear to be "leaning-in" on the videotape. A lens of 8 x 1 or 12 x 1 is usually sufficient for school video productions.

Most lenses have a macro lens installed within the lens. The macro lens allows the videographer to shoot extreme close-ups of small objects. A penny can be videotaped to fill the screen, or a giant eyeball can seem to leer at the viewer. With standard lenses, the minimum object distance is two to three feet, meaning that anything closer will not come into focus. With a standard 12 x 1 lens, an extreme close-up of a postage stamp will not come into focus, no matter how the focus ring is twisted. But a macro lens can easily perform this function! The lens should be put in the macro position for any videography under two to three feet.

The aperture is the opening in the lens that allows light to enter the camera body (figure 1.2). The lens is rarely "wide open." The size is often decreased by the lens iris, the mechanism that controls the aperture. In the light of a dozen candles at a sixth-grader's birthday party, the aperture is open quite wide. However, while videotaping on a sunny summer day, you can expect your iris to close the aperture down to the size of a pencil tip. Most video cameras and camcorders use lenses with automatic iris control, so the videographer generally doesn't have to worry about this. However, under certain circumstances, the videographer may want to override the automatic function, for example, if your subject is standing with the sun to her back. The automatic iris in the lens automatically keys onto the brightest part of the picture—the sun. Of course, your subject will now appear as a silhouette in a picture dominated by the bright, orange ball.

Fig. 1.2. Aperture of a lens.

> A *viewfinder* is a monochrome (black and white) monitor that displays the video picture that the camera is producing. Most viewfinders are actually of very high quality because the viewfinder screen is to close to the eye. As a comparison, briefly stand with your eye about three inches from a regular television screen while a video program is playing. See the difference? On the regular television screen, you probably see only a series of flashing dots. On the viewfinder, you see a complete, high-quality picture.

Most viewfinders are monochrome, however, some newer cameras feature color viewfinders. There is really very little advantage to having a color viewfinder, and it is basically a gimmick on consumer equipment. A viewfinder should be used to evaluate the picture composition, the shape of the items in a picture, and the amount of light in the picture. The presence of a color picture in the viewfinder distracts the camera operator from those objectives. If a video camera is in good condition and is properly white-balanced, the color trueness is not really a problem. If your cameras are already outfitted with color viewfinders, accept them and enjoy the luxury. However, a color viewfinder should not be considered a criterion for selecting a camera.

Many viewfinders display pertinent information about the camera or video deck's operation. By looking into the viewfinder, a videographer can often tell how much battery power is left, how much tape remains on the cassette, or if the proper amount of light is present, in addition to whether or not the video deck is actually recording. Because of space limitations, many of these functions are symbolically abbreviated. Consult your owner's manual for correct interpretation of these symbols.

Finally, when a video camera or camcorder won't operate correctly, check the viewfinder connection to the camera after determining that the camera is indeed getting power. Many embarrassed students have complained that their camcorders were broken, only to find that the viewfinder was disconnected.

> The *imaging device*, along with the electronic connections inside the camera body, converts the light collected by the lens into the video signal. The imaging device, therefore, is located within the camera body directly behind the lens. There are two types of imaging devices in cameras used today: 1) tubes and 2) charge-coupled devices (CCD).

When video cameras were invented in the 1920s they used heavy vacuum tubes, called camera pickup tubes, as imaging devices. The tube is a cylinder of glass that allows electrons to respond in a vacuum. Early tubes, such as Image-Orthicon, were quite large (about the size of an arm) and could get hot during long periods of operation. Although modern technology has eliminated these problems, the pickup tube is not without disadvantages. Tubes are expensive to replace and need attention during production. It is not uncommon for the colors to become distorted during a shoot. Because tube performance is temperamental, matching the color and brightness on two-tube cameras becomes an all-day task.

Most cameras made since the mid-1980s use CCDs for imaging devices. A CCD is a microchip stemming from the technology that gave us microcomputers. The CCD usually measures from ½ inch to 1 inch square. The CCD is divided into thousands of tiny areas called pixels. Each pixel is capable of interpreting that part of the light that comes from the lens. As you can imagine, the more pixels on the CCD, the higher the resolution of the television picture. Once again, though, modern technology allows us to cram a large number of pixels onto a very small CCD. The size of the CCD can no longer be the only factor in the resolution of the picture.

Most video cameras used in schools have a single tube or a single CCD. More professional cameras often employ up to three imaging devices. Three-tube/CCD cameras are the norm at television stations. The result of multiple imaging devices is, of course, a better-quality picture. The disadvantage is increased purchase and maintenance cost and brighter light requirements. That is why it is common to see a professional videographer using a portable light during the day. His or her professional camera requires a great deal of light to produce such a high-quality video signal.

> All of the elements that make up a video camera work together to make a useful tool for the videographer. A high-quality lens allows light to pass through bright and undistorted. A high-resolution imaging device produces a clean, clear video signal. And an accurate viewfinder gives the videographer a true representation of the video signal.

## The Tripod

A tripod should be used for many of your video productions. Tripods are light, portable camera supports that are relatively inexpensive and easy to use. A tripod can be set up in seconds and left standing for hours. Tripods provide a steady camera picture and tireless service. Tripods are strongly recommended for all advanced projects.

When choosing a tripod, make sure that it is designed for video camera use. Most tripods have weight limits; do not exceed them. Spending $20 or $30 more on a true video tripod is much cheaper than a costly repair of a lens or CCD.

## Audio Dub

Many camcorders and video decks have audio dub capability. To audio dub means to replace the old audio (sound) on a videotape with new audio. Even though most cameras/camcorders are stereo, most audio dubs erase and re-record both the left and right channels at once. A few of the more advanced models have split-channel capability. Audio dubbing is usually a matter of pressing the "audio-dub" button and the "play" button at the same time, much like you would push the "record" button and the "play" button of a tape recorder at the same time to record. However, the two functions must not be confused. When in the record function, the videotape recorder erases the video and audio channels and replaces the space on the tape with new video and audio signals. Even if no microphone is connected, the audio channel will be erased and replaced by a new signal; in this case no sound at all will be recorded. Let's suppose that you have videotaped several shots of your school and you wish to put the school song on the videotape. You currently have the school song on audiocassette. You can simply make a connection between the audio-out jack on the audiocassette deck and the audio-in jack on the videotape recorder. Then, by following the owner's manual, you can audio dub the school song onto the videotape, erasing any ambient sound you may have recorded at the time. If you accidentally press the "record" button instead of the "audio dub" button, you will erase the video and audio tracks. For a more convenient audio dub with less fidelity, you can use a microphone instead of the cord connection. Remember, the audio-dub function erases the existing audio and replaces it with new audio. The record function erases and replaces both video and audio, even if nothing is connected to the inputs.

The technology behind basic video production is actually quite simple to understand. As you continue your television production education, remember the concepts of television production that you have learned in this lesson.

## *Review Questions: Lesson 1*

1. The video camera takes in _____ and converts it into _____.

2. What is the main problem with a powerful telephoto lens?

3. What side effect is produced by a wide-angle lens?

4. What is the minimum camera-to-object distance for most lenses?

5. What should be done when the camera-to-object distance is closer than the minimum?

6. What type of information can be found in the camera viewfinder?

7. What two benefits are provided by a tripod?

8. Audio dubbing is replacing _____ with _____.

9. What happens if a videotape is audio dubbed, but no microphone is connected?

   *No sound is recorded – use other audio source (mic/cassette/CD, etc) and audio in jack to record new sound over video while taping or during editing*

## *Activities: Lesson 1*

1.  Ask a parent, grandparent, or community member about the differences between television now and television when he or she was young.

2.  Using microforms at your local library or school media center, find a magazine article about television production from the 1940s or 1950s.

3.  Visit a local television station and ask to see old photographs of the equipment that they used many years ago.

4.  Set your camera's zoom lens on its most telephoto setting. Make some videotape as you walk around campus. How does the tape differ from the same scenes recorded with the lens on the wide-angle setting?

5.  Brainstorm a list of 25 uses for a macro lens.

6.  Try making some videotape without using the viewfinder on your camera or camcorder.

# Student Project Plan: Macro-Lens Project

## DESCRIPTION OF COMPLETED PROJECT

The finished project will be a 2-minute videotape program consisting of 8-10 15-second shots of still photographs and a soundtrack that augments the content. The program will fade in on a hand-drawn title card and fade out on the last picture. Twenty seconds of black should precede and follow the project on the videotape.

## METHOD

1. Collect photographs that have a central theme.
2. Create a title card that reflects the content.
3. Videotape the photographs and the title card.
4. Audio dub the soundtrack.

## EQUIPMENT

video camera and deck or camcorder

tripod

monitor/television set

audio-dub system

## EVALUATION

The project will be worth 150 points:

photo selection    (25)

title card         (25)

camera work        (50)

fade-in and out    (25)

audio dub          (25)

## *Evaluation Sheet: Macro-Lens Project*

NAME _____

| | | |
|---|---|---|
| Photo selection | (25) | _____ |
| Title card | (25) | _____ |
| Camera work | (50) | _____ |
| Fade-in and fade-out | (25) | _____ |
| Audio dub | (25) | _____ |
| Point total | (150) | _____ |
| Letter grade | | A    B    C    D    Re-do |

**COMMENTS:**

# Lesson 2  Microphones for ENG Reporting and Videography

## Objectives

After successfully completing this lesson, you will be able to:

- *identify and describe the different types of microphones available to the television production interviewer.*

- *identify and describe the different pickup patterns available on microphones.*

- *exhibit the correct use of hand-held and lavaliere microphones.*

- *plan for an on-camera interview.*

- *identify possible topics for on-camera interviews.*

- *conduct a 1-minute on-camera interview, following an established format.*

- *videotape a single-shot, 1-minute interview.*

## Vocabulary

**Condenser microphone.** A microphone that generates audio signal by using air pressure to oscillate a diaphragm near a backplate. Condenser microphones require a power source.

**Dynamic microphone.** A microphone that generates audio signals by using air pressure to depress a magnetic coil.

**Electronic News Gathering (ENG).** The process of reporting timely events using basic videography equipment: a camera/deck system or camcorder, a microphone, earphones, and perhaps a light and tripod.

**Hand-held microphone.** A heavy-duty microphone designed to be used by an ENG reporter.

**Impedance.** Resistance to audio signal flow. Audio systems can be either high impedance (hi-Z) or low impedance (lo-Z).

**Lavaliere microphone.** A very small microphone (often called a tie-pin microphone).

**Omnidirectional pattern.** A microphone pickup pattern that allows the microphone to pick up sounds from every side of the microphone.

> **Shotgun microphone.** A microphone with a very narrow unidirectional pickup pattern.
>
> **Unidirectional pattern.** A microphone pickup pattern that picks up sound from only one side of the microphone. Also called the cardioid pattern.
>
> **Wireless microphone.** A microphone system that uses radio frequency instead of a microphone cord as a means to transport the audio signal from the microphone to the audio input on a camera or an audio mixer.

Not much news happens in a television studio. Sure, every once in a while a celebrity makes a startling revelation on a talk show. But by and large news happens in the real world. If television reporters are to report the news, they must learn to make quality television in the real world, outside of the studio.

## Electronic News Gathering (ENG)

No other part of a news program has the information, the drama, and the urgency of a reporter on the scene of a news event. This technique is known as electronic news gathering, or ENG. ENG is the process of reporting the news using the basic tools of the television trade: a camera/deck system or a camcorder, and a microphone. The tape rolls and the reporter and videographer try to convey the information and the atmosphere of the situation. The evening news is generally a series of ENG reports introduced by studio anchors.

ENG is different from electronic field production, or EFP. EFP involves taking more equipment into the field, in effect creating a small studio at the scene of the remote broadcast. Many top facilities have remote "trucks"—studios on wheels—that contain all of the equipment necessary for a complex EFP shoot. While EFP usually involves multiple camera setups, a switcher, graphics, and a great deal of planning, ENG is much more basic. An ENG team usually consists of a reporter and a videographer. Infrequently, a sound technician is added to record and monitor the audio. Sometimes the videographer is the only member of the ENG team, taping segments to be narrated by the anchor in the studio during the news program.

Because no producer or director is present, the ENG team must be self-reliant and self-directing. Successful ENG reporters must be knowledgeable in microphone technique in addition to their journalistic skills.

## Microphones

In Lesson 1, the video camera was defined as a device that converts light into electrical energy. A microphone is a device that converts sound into electrical energy. The electrical energy produced by a microphone is called the audio signal. The audio signal is then fed into the microphone jack on the camera or the video deck to be recorded simultaneously with the video (figure 1.3).

Elementary physics tells us that anything that makes a sound vibrates, and that vibration in the air travels to our ears and is converted back into the sound. A microphone, like the human ear, can also receive and interpret those sound waves. The part of the microphone that actually performs this function is the element of the microphone. A microphone element can be compared to a video imaging device in terms of function.

Two types of microphones are generally used in school-based ENG reporting: the dynamic microphone and the condenser microphone.

Fig. 1.3. Audio hookup to videocassette recorder.

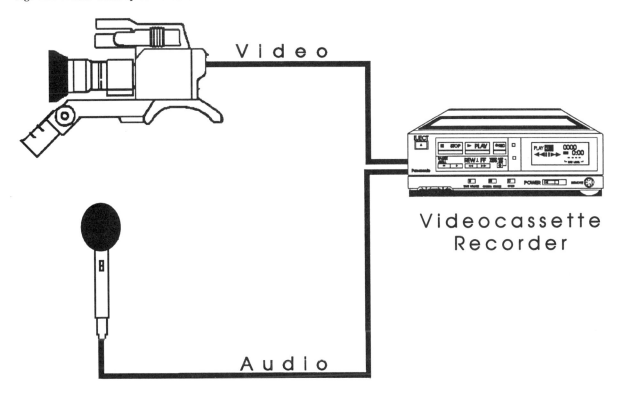

The *dynamic microphone* is the workhorse of school-based television production. Dynamic microphones are relatively inexpensive and quite durable. The dynamic microphone element consists of a diaphragm connected to a moving coil of wire. The sound waves collide with the diaphragm, causing the diaphragm to push against the coil. This push causes the coil to move up and down. It is this motion that produces the audio signal. Dynamic microphones offer moderate sound quality that falls well within the range of the needs of school-based television production. A dynamic microphone cannot, however, pick up the low bass and high treble sounds that we expect for high fidelity. Therefore, a dynamic microphone should be just fine for an interview with the assistant principal, but probably shouldn't be used to record the school orchestra.

The *condenser microphone* is higher in quality and is generally preferred by television professionals. A condenser microphone element consists of a diaphragm that vibrates in proximity to a backplate. It is this vibration that is converted into the audio signal. Condenser microphones give a good, flat response. The term "flat" in this case is good. A "flat" response means that the microphone responds well to high, medium, and low frequencies. If you were to draw a curve of the response, the curve would be flat on top, because the response is the same for all frequencies, or pitches (figure 1.4).

A condenser microphone needs its own power source to function. In most hand-held condenser microphones, the power supply comes from a battery within the microphone. Battery size can range from hearing-aid size to 9 volt, depending on the microphone. Because these condenser microphones provide their own power supplies, they are called electret condenser microphones. Some condenser microphones, especially those designed for television or music studios, get their power from the audio mixer. This power provided by the mixer is called "phantom power." Higher-quality audio mixers usually have a switch labeled "phantom power." With that switch in the "on" position, nonelectret condenser microphones, also known as "true" condenser microphones, will get their required power supply directly from the audio mixer. Condenser microphones are more expensive than dynamic microphones, but the investment is worth it, especially for schools with elaborate television production departments or videographers who regularly tape events that require high-fidelity audio.

Fig. 1.4. Curve of a microphone flat response.

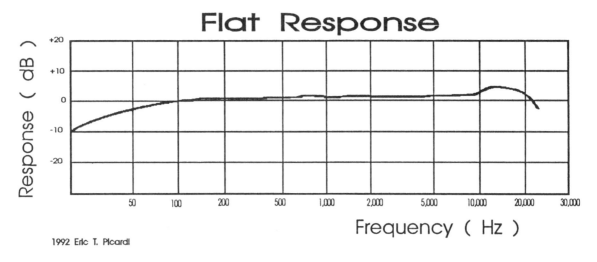

1992 Eric T. Picardi

## Microphone Pickup Patterns

Not all microphones process sound waves in the same way. Also, not all microphones receive sound from all areas of the environment. The area of the environment from which the microphone receives sound waves is called the microphone pickup pattern. Figure 1.5 illustrates the two major pickup patterns: the omnidirectional pattern and the unidirectional, or cardioid, pattern.

Fig. 1.5. Microphone pickup patterns.

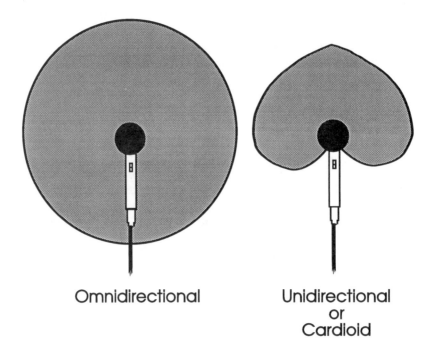

*Omnidirectional microphones* pick up sound from all directions, as the name implies. An omnidirectional microphone could be placed in the middle of a singing quartet standing in a circle. Each singer's voice would be recorded equally well. Omnidirectional microphones are great for collecting ambient, or environmental, sound. A videographer making a tape of the scenery at a park could use an omnidirectional microphone to simultaneously record the sounds of the babbling brook, the chirping birds, and the children playing catch on the playground. Omnidirectional microphones can also be used for interviews, as long as the ambient noise is at a minimum. But if an airplane flies overhead or a fire truck zooms by, say good-bye to the audio of the interview subject. The omnidirectional microphone will pick up evenly all sounds within its range.

The microphone most frequently used in interviews is the *unidirectional microphone.* A unidirectional microphone receives sound from the top much more than from the sides or back. The pattern is heart-shaped, with the microphone being in between the lobes of the heart shape, pointing toward the point. It is for this reason that the unidirectional microphone is often called a cardioid microphone. Cardioid microphones are used whenever a specific sound source needs to be recorded. Of course, when the sound source changes, the microphone direction must be changed. If an interviewer uses a cardioid microphone, she must change the direction of the microphone each time a different person speaks. A cardioid microphone can be called a "sound flashlight" because it must be pointed at the source of the sound. If our interviewer continuously pointed the cardioid microphone at herself throughout the interview, the comments of her guests would be barely audible.

Cardioid microphones can vary in their degree of pickup pattern narrowness. A cardioid microphone with an extremely narrow pickup pattern is called a shotgun microphone (figure 1.6). Shotgun microphones can be used when the source is a moderate distance from the audio technician. For example, let's say that your science teacher is demonstrating an experiment and you are videotaping the experiment for other classes to watch. You could mount a shotgun microphone to your camera or camcorder to record the teacher's description of the experiment. Terms used to describe very narrow pickup patterns have included super-cardioid, hyper-cardioid, and ultra-cardioid. Some more expensive microphones have a three-way switch that allows you to choose the narrowness of the pickup pattern. Testing the shotgun microphone beforehand can best describe the characteristics of your particular cardioid microphone.

Fig. 1.6. Shotgun microphone.

## Using Omnidirectional and Unidirectional Microphones

As with the camera, the quality of the audio signal depends on the type of microphone you have and its proper use. A great microphone, used improperly, will produce a poor audio signal. The general rule is speak *across* the top of an omnidirectional microphone and *into* a unidirectional microphone.

## Determining Which Microphone to Use

Each microphone fits into two of the four categories listed above. A microphone is either dynamic or condenser, and either omnidirectional or cardioid. Therefore, most microphones fit into one of the following four combination categories:

dynamic omnidirectional

dynamic cardioid

condenser omnidirectional

condenser cardioid.

Unfortunately, the size and shape of the microphone has nothing to do with its element or its pickup pattern. A dynamic omnidirectional microphone could be identical to a condenser cardioid microphone. But as you know, the microphones are very different. Consult the owner's manual before you use the microphone. Don't be fooled by appearance.

## Microphones for Special Situations

Up to this point, we have specifically referred to hand-held or camera-mounted microphones. Two other types of microphones are available to school-based videographers: lavaliere microphones and wireless microphones.

*Lavaliere microphones*, commonly called "tie-pin" microphones, are very small and lightweight (figure 1.7). Since the inception of television, on-camera talent have wanted a microphone that could travel around the studio with them and still leave their hands free. Early television instructional

**Fig. 1.7. Lavaliere, or tie-pin, microphone.**

**Fig. 1.8. Lavaliere battery pack.**

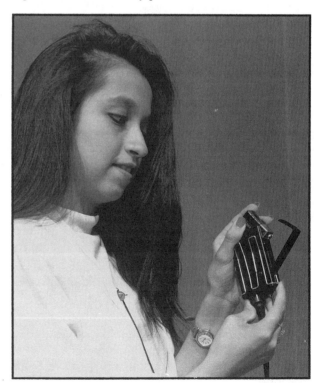

programs show a chef cooking in a kitchen with a hand-held microphone tied around his neck with a rope or chain; lavaliere microphones are a smaller version of this early technology. Now professional lavaliere microphones can be as small as a hat pin, and still deliver full-frequency response. Lavaliere microphones are surprisingly affordable to schools, costing about as much as a good hand-held dynamic microphone. However, a lavaliere is definitely a one-source microphone. Each person must have his or her own lavaliere. (This can get tricky when a camera has only one or two microphone input jacks.) Lavaliere microphones are usually condenser omnidirectional. Because the lavaliere is so small, a hearing aid battery is usually used for the power source. Some lavalieres run a thin cord from the microphone to a power supply about 2 inches square into which a 9-volt battery is inserted (figure 1.8). This battery pack can be attached to the belt or put in a pocket. Lavalieres can be very useful when hands-free performance is desired.

*Wireless microphones* are used in television production when running a line of microphone cable is impractical or impossible. Wireless microphones, as the name indicates, do not use microphone cable to connect the microphone to the video camera or audio mixer. Instead, a broadcasted FM signal is used. A wireless microphone system consists of three components: the microphone, the transmitter, and the receiving station (figure 1.9). The microphone can be either hand-held or lavaliere. The transmitter produces and broadcasts the FM radio signal, just like a small radio station. (Usually, the signal is well above the FM dial.) The transmitter for the hand-held wireless microphone is usually installed within the microphone itself. In the lavaliere wireless microphone, the transmitter is usually a small plastic box worn on the belt that is connected to the lavaliere microphone with a thin, lightweight cable. The receiving station is nothing more than a high-quality radio receiver tuned specifically to the frequency broadcasted by that particular wireless microphone. Some of the receiving stations can be tuned to different frequencies, but the majority affordable to school-based video facilities will have manufacturer pretuned receiving stations.

Fig. 1.9. A wireless microphone system.

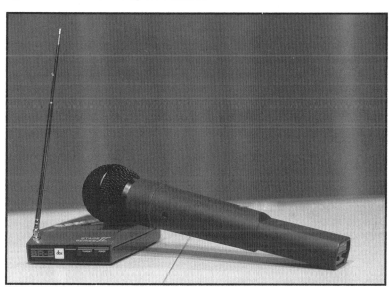

Wireless microphones are frequently used in talk shows and variety shows to allow the talent to move about without worrying about snagging or stumbling over the microphone cable. A singer could stand at midfield to sing the national anthem before a football game. The possibilities are endless. A broken microphone cable is indeed a frustrating experience. Let's say your school has arranged for a prominent member of the community to come to speak to all of the 10th graders who have gathered in the auditorium. Your assignment is to videotape the presentation so that the entire student body can watch it. In order to get a good long shot and a good close-up, you position your camera on a tripod about 10 rows, or 40 feet, from the stage. Your microphone is positioned at the lectern next to the microphone for the public address system. If you have a wireless microphone, you simply plug the receiving station into the microphone jack on your camera (figure 1.10). If you are using a traditional microphone, you must string a microphone cable through the rows and connect it to the camera. For safety's sake, the cable must be taped to the floor, but still you run the risk of damaging the cable as 400 sophomores trample through. The wireless system is obviously more convenient in this situation.

Fig. 1.10. Wireless microphone connection.

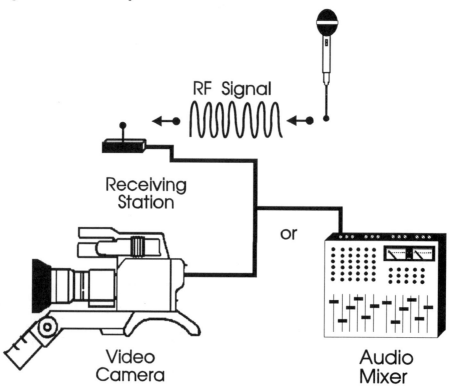

Wireless microphone systems are not without their disadvantages. The most obvious is cost. A medium-quality wireless microphone system costs about $300. That's a lot of videotape! In order to function properly, a wireless microphone should have a direct line of sight with the receiving station. Trees, brick walls, and fences have been associated with poor wireless performance. Adverse weather conditions can also hamper use. A proximity of high-voltage equipment, such as theater lights, can also distort the sound.

Obviously, investing in an expensive system requires careful thought. The range, or transmitting distance, is a significant consideration. Recently, a small consumer video-oriented business offered a wireless microphone system for only $49.95. Unfortunately, the range of transmission was only 35 feet! That much microphone cable can be purchased for about $10. More professional systems offer ranges from 500-1,000 feet. But remember, the environment is everything. High voltage in the area can cut range by more than 50 percent. The frequency is also an important consideration. Wireless microphone frequencies can vary from 48 mHz (megahertz) to 200 mHz. Generally speaking, the higher the frequency the better. Forty-nine mHz is generally used for toy walkie-talkies. Purchasing that $49.95 model would give you a tinny, poor-quality sound. About 170 mHz is the professional range. Make sure that your wireless microphone will give you a professional sound.

Other wireless microphone criteria include the presence of cross-frequencies, and the quality of the microphone itself. A wireless microphone receiver cannot discriminate between the intended signal and any other signals of the same frequency in the area. Here's an example: A principal is using a lavaliere microphone that broadcasts at 49 mHz while giving a speech to the student body. The auditorium technical crew is operating the lights and raising and lowering the curtain. They are using wireless walkie-talkies that also use a frequency of 49 mHz. Imagine the embarrassment when the cue "Dim the lights" comes over the public address system! The wireless microphone receiving station has received both the principal's signal and the technical crew's communications.

Most wireless microphone companies offer a number of different frequencies, or "channels," for purchase. For example, let's say you are responsible for mixing the music for a quartet of singers. Should they all use the same frequencies for their wireless microphones? That's up to you, and there are advantages and disadvantages to each choice. If they each use the same channel, you could use one receiving station to receive all four singers. This is fine, unless one singer is singing too loudly, and another is singing too softly. With one frequency, you could not adjust the volume within the frequency. In this case, the choice might be to go with four separate microphone channels. However, this can get very expensive.

It would be nice if all wireless microphone systems included high-quality microphones. But, unfortunately, they don't. When considering the use of a wireless system, evaluate the microphone as if you were selecting it on its own merit. Range and frequency mean nothing if the microphone itself is of poor quality.

Wireless microphones are certainly impressive and convenient, but they aren't a panacea. Their use often raises more questions than answers, and their merits and demerits should be carefully considered before purchase.

## Microphone Use

Ideally, the correct microphone placement is 6 to 8 inches from the source (figure 1.11). This placement allows for the recording of a source, and not just a general area. When an area is miked, background noise often plays a prominent role. Whenever possible, the audio technician should try to record the source of the sound.

Hand-held microphones should be held at about chest level, unless a great deal of ambient noise is present. The noisier the area, the closer the microphone should be to the mouth. For example, if a student is reporting from a quiet park, the 6- to 8-inch rule applies. If, however, a segment is recorded during a noisy pep rally, the microphone should be held closer to the lips.

A windscreen is recommended for all outdoor microphone uses. Many professionals use windscreens all the time to enhance and standardize the microphone appearance. A windscreen is simply a piece of foam rubber shaped to fit over the head of the microphone. The windscreen effectively muffles any rumble or whistle caused by breezes, while allowing the desired sound to pass through undistorted. Windscreens are more important for omnidirectional microphones. Because the omnidirectional collects sound from all areas, it is more likely to catch the direction of the wind. Windscreens can be purchased at most audio and electronics supply stores. A simple generic windscreen can be purchased for less than $2. Windscreens custom-made to the size of your microphone will cost more. However, the investment pays for itself on the first windy day.

Fig. 1.11. Correct microphone placement.

Experience is the key to effective microphone use. Even microphones of the same make and model may perform differently in the field. Knowing the particulars of each microphone in your collection can help maintain high quality throughout your video production.

## Microphone Impedance

A microphone for use in a school can be either high or low impedance. The term *impedance* refers to the amount of resistance to the audio signal flow. High-impedance (Hi-Z) microphones are used in consumer and some professional situations. Low-impedance (Lo-Z) microphones are used in professional and broadcast situations. A distinction must be made because the two systems are not compatible.

High-impedance microphones can be used only with high-impedance systems, including camera jacks and audio mixers. The maximum cable length for high-impedance systems is about 35 feet. After that, the signal becomes weak and distorted. High-impedance systems generally do not sound as clear as low-impedance systems.

Low-impedance microphone systems are used in professional and broadcast productions. Cable length can go up to 1,000 feet, and the quality is generally clearer.

Most schools will use high-impedance systems. Because low-impedance systems are more professional, they usually cost more. Some schools with elaborate television facilities will have low-impedance systems in their studios, but these studio microphones may not be compatible with the cameras used for ENG work.

Microphones can be changed from high to low or low to high impedance by using an impedance adaptor. Impedance adaptors are available from most electronics and audio stores and cost around $20. Some microphones have switchable impedance for use with either impedance system.

High-impedance microphones usually have ¼-inch "headphone-type" jacks as connectors, while low-impedance systems usually use three-pronged XLR connectors. The operative word here is "usually." While the rule makes common sense, it is not always applied. Of course, any electrician can change the connector for a nominal charge.

Audio is certainly a critical part of ENG reporting. With a correct knowledge of microphone types and their uses, an ENG team can venture into the "real world" to bring the news to everyone.

## *Review Questions: Lesson 2*

1. Define the following terms:

   ENG


   EFP


2. What is the difference between ENG and EFP?


3. A microphone converts sound waves into _____.


4. Which type of microphone requires a power source?


5. Where does "phantom power" come from?


6. A microphone with a very narrow pickup pattern is called a _____.


7. What situations can have a negative effect on the range of a wireless microphone system?


8. What is the correct placement for a hand-held microphone?

# *Activities: Lesson 2*

1.  Call a local television station or production facility and ask for a tour of an EFP truck. Report to the class.

2.  Ask the local television station about the requirements for the positions of ENG reporter and videographer.

3.  Videotape several ENG reports from your local newscast. What types of microphones do they use?

4.  Compare television news coverage of events to the newspaper stories on the same events. How are they similar? How are they different?

5.  Ask parents, grandparents, or community members how television ENG coverage has changed through the years.

6.  Research the history of microphones. What types of microphones (other than condenser and dynamic) have been used in the past?

# *Student Project Plan: Interview Project*

## DESCRIPTION OF COMPLETED PROJECT

The finished project will be a 1-minute interview with anyone who comes to this school on a daily basis. The video will consist of a two-shot/bust shot, and the audio will be the actual interview.

## METHOD

1. Students select the job they want: interviewer or videographer.
2. Students select a partner and form a team.
3. Team selects a person to interview.
4. Interview is scheduled with guest.
5. Interview is videotaped.
6. Team views and critiques videotape.
7. Videotapes are shown to the class and evaluated by the teacher.

## EQUIPMENT

camcorder or camera/deck system

hand-held microphone

headphones

## EVALUATION

The project will be worth 150 points:

Interviewer:

| | |
|---|---|
| microphone technique | (20) |
| quality of questions | (20) |
| camera presence (eye contact, posture, etc.) | (20) |
| format/script | (15) |

Videographer:

| | |
|---|---|
| proper shot | (20) |
| steady shot | (20) |
| 15 seconds before and after | (20) |
| background/location | (15) |

General Impression (75)—same for each team member

## *Sample Format/Script: Interview Project*

(Total time—1 minute)

Hello. Our guest today on _____ is _____.
show (series) name                    name of guest

_____ is _____.
name of guest          why you are interviewing this guest

Questions and answers.

Thank you, _____. For _____,
name of guest                  show (series) name

I'm _____.
interviewer's name

- - - - - - - - - - - - - - - - - - - - - - - - - - - - - - - - - - - - - - - - - - - - - - - -

Hello. Our guest today on "Meet the Panthers" is Coach Tom
Carlsen. Coach Carlsen is our head football coach here at Dr.
Phillips High School.

Questions and Answers.

Thank you, Coach Carlsen. For "Meet the Panthers," I'm
Joe Student.

## *Evaluation Sheet: Interview Project*

**INTERVIEWER** _____

| | | |
|---|---|---|
| Microphone technique | (20) | _____ |
| Quality of questions | (20) | _____ |
| Camera presence (eye contact, posture, etc.) | (20) | _____ |
| Format/script | (15) | _____ |
| Subtotal—Interviewer | (75) | _____ |

**VIDEOGRAPHER** _____

| | | |
|---|---|---|
| Proper shot | (20) | _____ |
| Steady shot | (20) | _____ |
| 15 seconds before and after | (20) | _____ |
| Background/location | (15) | _____ |
| Subtotal—videographer | (75) | _____ |
| General Impression | (75) | _____ |

**COMMENTS:**

Interviewer   _____ + _____ = _____
               individual      team      total

Videographer   _____ + _____ = _____
               individual      team      total

# Lesson 3   Postproduction Basics

## Objectives

After successfully completing this lesson, you will be able to:

- *use an audio mixer.*
- *recognize and select appropriate audio sources and microphones.*
- *write quality scripts for video production.*
- *select an electronic character generator for the production situation.*
- *compose graphics for television production.*

## Vocabulary

**Audio mixer.** An electronic device that allows selection, combination, and amplification of various audio inputs.

**Automatic gain control (AGC).** In audio, a feature that automatically adjusts the audio level to the correct setting.

**Cart.** An audio playback cartridge. A cart is an endless loop of tape wrapped around a hub that provides continuous playback.

**Cart machine.** A machine that plays and records carts.

**Character generator.** An electronic device that creates typed letters and displays them on a video screen for use and recording.

**Cue.** Has two meanings: 1) to set an audio source to the desired point, as in "cue a tape" and 2) a feature on many audio mixers that allows for cuing of an audio source without sending that source out through the master output.

**Equalization.** The process of adjusting the relative strengths of the audio frequencies. Equalization usually includes separate controls for high, mid-range, and low tones.

**Fader.** A slide used to control the input level of an audio source.

**Feedback.** The loud squealing sound emitted from a speaker when a microphone "hears itself."

**Font.** A type style used in character generation.

**Postproduction.** Video or audio work for the television program that takes place after the original recording.

**Potentiometer.** A dial that controls input level on an audio mixer.

**Trim potentiometer.** A dial that fine-tunes and calibrates the input fader or potentiometer.

**Voice talent.** Has two meanings: 1) the narration performance and 2) the narration performer. Example: 1) "Our audio-dub consists of music and voice talent" and 2) "The voice talent needs to speak into the microphone."

**Volume unit (VU) meter.** An analog or LED instrument that measures input- and output-level intensity.

ENG is great for simple interviews and news reports. But sometimes television programs require more audio and video than can be possibly or practically created at the site of the original recording. Video or audio work for the television program after the original recording is called postproduction. Postproduction often includes editing, electronic special effects, and digitization. But for our purposes in beginning television production, postproduction consists of audio-dubbing music and script and adding graphics.

## Audio Postproduction Equipment

An audio mixer is a device that allows the operator to select, combine, and amplify different audio sources. In its simplest form, an audio mixer could be a switch that selects an audio source. Complex audio mixers are found in recording studios, where dozens of voices and instruments can be combined onto a single tape. Most audio mixers used in television production fall somewhere in between, and it is to that level that this lesson is geared.

Generally, all audio that goes into the videotape recorder during the audio-dubbing process comes through the audio mixer (figure 1.12). Therefore, all microphones and recorded sound sources should be connected to the mixer. For a simple audio dub with narration and music, only a microphone and tape/compact disc (CD) player would need to be connected to the mixer's inputs. For a more complex audio dub, with three narrators, music, sound effects, and voice from another videotaped interview, the technician would probably connect three microphones, an audiotape cassette player, a CD player, and a videotape player to the mixer. Therefore, when selecting a mixer, the technician should consider the most complex project to be completed on the equipment.

The microphones and audio sources mentioned above are connected to the

Fig. 1.12. Audio mixer.

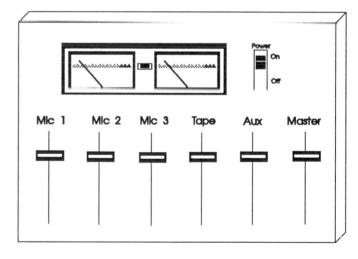

inputs of the mixer. The inputs for the microphones are generally labeled "MIC" or "M1, M2," etc. Simple mixers accommodate up to three microphones; more complex mixers may accommodate 16 different microphones. Whether the mixer can handle 1 or 100 microphones, it is important to remember that each narrator or voice talent participating in the audio-dub process should have his or her own microphone. For that reason, it is a good idea to have an audio mixer with a few more microphone inputs than you typically need.

A unidirectional (cardioid) microphone is usually best for an audio dub. The cardioid mic allows for single-source recording, and can eliminate recording of most quiet to moderate background noise. An omnidirectional microphone can be used, as long as all voice talent not currently speaking are quiet.

While microphones for voice talent are used to convey specific information, the general tone of the video program can be greatly influenced by the recorded music and sound effects integrated into the audio-dub process through the mixer. Most audio mixers have inputs for audiocassette tape players, CD players, videotape players (audio tracks only), and other, less-frequently used sources. Once again, plan for the most saturated use of your equipment, and then add one or two inputs for those unexpected situations to determine the number of audio inputs needed on your console.

Audiocassette tapes offer an inexpensive, professional source of recorded music for television programs. The audiocassette input on the mixer is usually labeled "tape" or "tape in." The owner's manual can help if the simple connection does not produce the desired result. Music is the source generally associated with audiocassette. But a large library of sound effects can be purchased or recorded on audiocassette, and personal interviews or field recordings where only audio is desired can be recorded on audiocassette and integrated into the audio-dub process through the mixer.

CD players revolutionized audio playback for video programs. The sound is crisper than its cassette cousin. But the boon for the CD player in video applications has been the instantaneous location of a single track on the CD. When the on-camera or voice talent makes a mistake, re-cuing the music on compact disc is usually as simple as pushing a button. And because each track on a CD is time-indexed for each second, an audio technician can re-cue to the middle of a song with ease.

CDs have also made recorded sound effects easier to access and use. Locating a sound effect on a phonograph record can be tedious. Often, a single $33\frac{1}{3}$ phonograph record contains 50 sound effects, forcing even the best audio technicians to stick a penlight in their mouth and a magnifying glass in their hand while trying to find the right track. Because the process must be repeated each time the director needs the effect, the result is often scratched records and frustrated students. One hundred sound effects can be recorded on a single CD, and they can be accessed simply by entering the correct number on the CD player. Because most CD players have auto-repeat functions, the sound effect can be repeated throughout the audio dub with ease. For example, let's say you're audio-dubbing a documentary about the circus, and you would like to combine circus sounds with your narration on the audio dub. You locate the appropriate track "circus sounds" on the sound effects CD. However, the desired effect lasts only a minute and your video program is three minutes. You can program the CD player to repeat the "circus sounds" continuously so that the sound effect is seamless throughout the audio dub.

Unfortunately, we are still a few years away from recordable compact discs on the consumer/ school level. However, the technology is being developed by several companies. Although it may be a few years before the technology is affordable to schools, rest assured that in the future, compact discs will be considered equal to audiocassettes in terms of recording. The CD player is usually connected to the mixer through the "aux" (auxiliary) jack. A CD player can be connected through a "tape in" or "phono" (phonograph) jack, however, the audio technician should expect to keep the level lower than expected because the CD player generally has a higher output signal level than an audiocassette player or a phonograph. With CD players coming down in price to the level of audiocassette decks, most schools are adding them to their basic audio systems.

Very few phonograph records are being pressed today. The phonograph record continued to thrive in spite of the popularity of the audiocassette format, but the compact disc rendered it obsolete. Except for special dance records used in discoteques and dance clubs, the phonograph is destined to go the way of the 8-track tape—a technology that was useful and popular but has been replaced by a more dependable and portable medium. Schools still buy and use turntables (record players) although the practice will probably die out altogether within the next few years as records accumulate scratches and become warped and worn. Still, many television production instructors own a cache of "classic" (i.e., pre-1990) records that students might find amusing to run over ending credits on the school news show. Most audio mixers have inputs for phonographs, and some mixers distinguish between ceramic phonograph systems and magnetic systems. Connection in the wrong input usually produces unusable audio, so if your turntable is ceramic and your mixer will only accept magnetic turntables, you'll need to buy a preamplifier for the turntable to make it compatible with the mixer.

Other audio sources are used infrequently in television. Sound from a videotape program can be used for an audio dub. For example, let's say your school is beginning a recycling program. You have a videotape interview of the principal explaining the specifics of the new program. You also have a videotape that shows students collecting aluminum around the school, placing it in the recycling bins, and loading it into a truck for delivery to the recycling center. The audio portion of the first videotape (principal interview) can be used as your narration for the audio dub of your second tape (aluminum collection). Simply run a cable from the audio "out" jack of a VCR containing the principal interview tape into the "tape in" or "aux" jack of your audio mixer. Also, connect a video monitor to the first VCR (principal interview) so that you can establish some sort of visual cue as to when to un-pause the first tape. Then, at the appropriate time, un-pause the first VCR and let the principal interview serve as your "voice talent."

Cart machines are also used infrequently in video productions. Cart machines work like 8-track tape players and are similar in appearance (figure 1.13). Carts are tapes wound as an endless loop around a hub in the middle. Therefore, because the tape has no beginning or end, the tape plays forever without stopping. Carts are used for theme music or introductions that are likely to be repeated on a regular basis. Radio stations record most of their commercials on carts. A special inaudible "beep" can be recorded on the cart at the beginning of the song or commercial. This "sync tone" stops the tape right before the song is about to start again. For example, let's say that your school news show uses 45 seconds of the same song as an opening every day. If you have a cart machine, you can record that song onto a 60-second cart. The recording process usually automatically records that "sync tone" right before the song starts. Every day, your 45-second song plays on the cart and then the cart continues to run silently for another 15 seconds (remember, you used a 60-second cart). Right before the song starts again, the cart stops, ready for the next time you push the "play" button on the cart machine.

Fig. 1.13. Cart machine.

You can see why carts are so popular at radio stations. Most radio stations play about 50 or 60 different commercials each day, and the carts eliminate endless cuing of tapes while allowing local production. In the TV studio, the cart has been replaced by—you guessed it—the CD. Just like the videotape player, the cart machine can usually be connected to the "tape in" or "aux" inputs of your mixer.

## The Audio Mixer: A Closer Look

As you can see, the audio mixer is important for connecting and combining several audio sources, and no studio could work without one. However, an audio mixer is more than just a series of connections. Mixers generally have a series of controls that display the intensity of the sound and shape the sound to the needs of the producer.

The level, or intensity, of the sound being input into the mixer is controlled by a potentiometer ("pot") or a fader (figure 1.14). A pot is a dial that controls the sound level. A knob on a car stereo that increases the volume is a pot. Pots are used as level controls on older mixers. Pots are still used in the

Fig. 1.14. Potentiometer.

"sound-shaping" part of the mixer, so they can't be discounted. But the major drawback to using pots for level controls lies in their difficulty of operation. A two-handed audio technician can reasonably adjust only two input pots. Enter the fader (or slider) bar (figure 1.15). Most modern mixers use fader bars to control each input's volume intensity. A fader bar is a sliding version of the potentiometer, with the lower end (bottom) indicating zero input and the upper end (top) indicating maximum input. The correct position is usually somewhere in between. Fader bars are just as accurate as pots, and many faders can be moved at once by adept audio technicians. Almost all mixers manufactured today use fader bars to control audio input intensity.

Fig. 1.15. Fader bar.

But how does the audio technician know how far to move the pots or faders? Certainly the mixer has an upper limit, after which the signal becomes distorted. The audio technician's useful tool is called a VU, or volume unit, meter. A VU meter shows the audio technician the level, or intensity, of the sound entering the audio mixer (figure 1.16). A VU meter is usually labeled -20 to +3. The zero represents 100 percent of the mixer's capability. For convenience, the VU meter is also labeled "0% to 100%," usually along the bottom of the meter. The audio technician should keep the VU meter level below the 0 level (100 percent). If the meter gives a higher reading, the audio will become distorted.

Fig. 1.16. Volume unit (VU) meter settings.

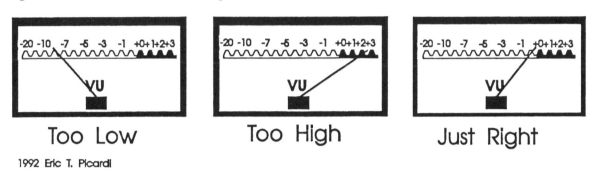

Too Low          Too High          Just Right

1992 Eric T. Picardi

If the VU meter does not approach the 100 percent mark at least every once in a while, the input is set too low, and the sound will be thin and weak, not rich and full. Most VU meters print the area over 100 percent in red ink, and the lower, acceptable area in black. Therefore, a good rule is "the level should approach the red, but not go into it."

The classic VU meter is a needle moving across a graduated background, like a speedometer on a car. But just as cars have turned to LED technology, VU meters can also use LED. LED stands for light-emitting diode. A LED is simply an electronic diode that produces light when a current is passed through it. The audio technician with a LED VU meter simply observes the area that is lit, in comparison to the printed graduate on the side. For ease of use, the lights under 100 percent are usually green, and the lights at and above 100 percent are red. Therefore, the technician simply avoids a continuous stream of red lights. (A color-blind audio technician generally experiences difficulty with a LED VU meter.) Which is better, a dial (analog) VU meter or a LED VU meter? It really depends on the preference of the audio technician. Professional recording studios are often equipped with analog VU meters, but LED is making its effect felt. Because of the constant display of the dial, the analog meter is considered more professional and reliable. After all, a single LED burnout could cause the technician to overadjust the audio, resulting in distortion.

Adjusting a VU meter for a single source is really quite simple. As the music plays or the announcer speaks, the technician simply adjusts the fader or pot to the correct level ("approaching the red, but not going into it"). But what if the audio dub calls for narration and music? Can each source (microphone and tape player) be adjusted independently before the audio dub? No. Volume units are additive—they combine within the mixer. Therefore, a separate pot or fader is usually located on the right side of the mixer and labeled "master." The master output controls the intensity of the final mix produced by the audio mixer. Let's return to our simple example above. A student wants to audio dub using voice narration on microphone 1 and music on a CD player plugged into the "aux" jack on the mixer. The audio technician, wearing headphones plugged into the headphone jack of the audio mixer, plays the CD and asks the narrator to begin reading the script. The technician adjusts the two faders "mic 1" and "aux") so that the mix sounds good—the voice is the dominant part and the music provides a nice background. But the VU meters are still very low. The technician slides the master fader bar up until the VU meter approaches the red, but doesn't go into it. The master control, then, controls the intensity of the final signal being sent from the mixer.

Some audio mixers have automatic gain control or AGC. As its name indicates, AGC automatically adjusts the level on the VU meters for optimum performance. This feature is also available on many higher-quality VCRs. AGC sounds like a dream come true for audio technicians, no more worrying about the correct level. However, AGC is not without its problems. An audio mixer is useful, but it's not smart. Mixers cannot distinguish a soft piano solo from a heavy-metal anthem. All audio is automatically adjusted to the highest level. So while AGC can prevent amateurish catastrophes, it cannot interpret the subtlety required for advanced video projects.

Sometimes, especially with high-powered CD players or loud narrators, the fader bar cannot be placed low enough. With the fader bar at the very bottom, no sound passes through. But the slightest upward movement causes input overload. Conversely, a narrator with a quiet voice might not be able to move the VU meter satisfactorily. For this reason, most high-quality mixers are equipped with trim potentiometers, or "trim pots" for each audio input (figure 1.17). In the cases listed above, the audio technician could adjust the trim pot so that each audio input could be adequately adjusted within the physical range of the fader bar. Think of the trim pot as a calibration of the fader bar.

**Fig. 1.17. Trim potentiometers.**

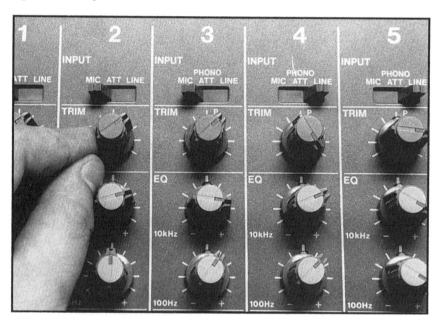

"Cue" is another function found on some audio mixers. Cue allows the audio technician to hear a source before selecting it. For this reason, each audio input has its own cue button. Here's an example. During a 10-minute talk show, an audio technician would like to use two songs from the same audiocassette: song number 1 for the opening theme and song number 2 for the ending credits. In this situation, the audio technician has limited choices: He could hook up a second cassette deck next door, and cue up the tape out of earshot of the talk show hosts and guests, or he could use the counter on the audiocassette player, which is only marginally accurate. Our audio technician could easily use the cue button on his mixer. The cue button above the audiocassette fader is pressed, and the fader itself is left down, so that the sound of the next song being cued does not become part of the master audio output. But as the cue button is pressed, the sound of the audiocassette player comes through the headphone jack of the mixer. Once the closing song is properly cued, the audio technician presses the cue button back to its original position, and the headphones return to the master output. The cue button is quite useful for cuing music during a video production.

Some of the more elaborate mixers have built-in equalization, or EQ. EQ is a complex version of the treble/bass selection on most consumer stereo systems. EQ on a mixer is usually controlled by a series of pots directly above the fader of the input to be equalized. There are usually three EQ pots: one for treble (high notes), one for midrange, and one for bass. By manipulating these EQ pots, the audio technician can shape the sound being sent through the mixer. Narrators can be given rich bass sounds. The sound of a hand-held AM radio can be simulated by turning the treble and midrange pots all the way up and turning the bass EQ pot all the way down. Creative technicians can find many uses for EQ. A word of advice about EQ: Beware of decreasing the EQ pots below midpoint. Once the sound is taken out, it cannot be put back in. For that reason, EQ should be used carefully in video projects to be played back many times in different situations.

## Audio Mixer/VCR Connections

The audio mixer must be properly connected to the VCR used for recording/audio dubbing. This is really quite simple. Main outputs, usually labeled "main out" or "master out" are located on the back of the mixer. If your mixer is stereo, there will be two jacks. A shielded cable can be used to connect those outputs to the audio input ("audio in") of the VCR. Once again, if the VCR is stereo, there should be two input jacks. For mono (single-audio channel) VCRs, only one audio input jack will be present. In that case, you have two options. One is to change the mixer from stereo to mono, if that option is given to you. This is usually accomplished with the flip of a switch located near the master output fader. A second option is to purchase a Y-connector at your local electronics supply company. The two output cables from your mixer should be plugged into the Y-connector, and the single output is then connected to the "audio-in" jack on the mono VCR. The first option is obviously simpler, but the mono/stereo switch might not be provided on your mixer. Figure 1.18 illustrates a proper audio/video connection.

Fig. 1.18. Audio/video connection.

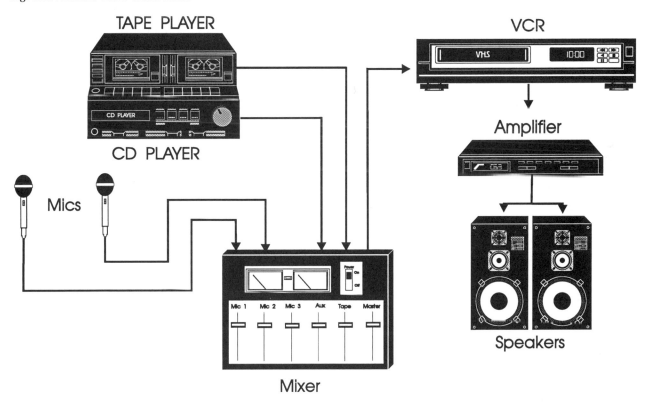

Many of the top VCRs have their own audio input level faders/pots and their own VU meters. The VCR is simply allowing another adjustment for audio input. Adjust the faders/pots on the VCR using the VU meters just as you would the master level on the audio mixer. Make sure to check your VCR to see if it has its own input level. Failure to adjust this level can result in poor-quality audio recording.

After the "audio out" of the mixer is connected to the "audio in" of the VCR and all levels are properly set, quality recording should take place. But what if an audience would like to hear the audio being recorded? The obvious answer is to connect a television to the "RF OUT" ("OUT to TV") on the VCR used for recording. The audio and video are then available to the audience. If a larger audience would like to hear the audio, then the VCR can be connected to an audio amplifier. Most electronic dealers carry simple audio amplifiers at a moderate price. A connection is made from the "audio out" of the VCR to the "tape in" of the amplifier. Once this connection is made and a set of speakers is connected to the amplifier, a roomful of students can hear the audio dub in progress. Notice that this is the first time in the audio process that an amplifier and speakers have been used. Remember the correct configuration: audio sources into the mixer; mixer into the VCR for recording; VCR into the amplifier for loudness control; amplifier into the speakers for large audience output. Of course, the recording of audio can take place without the amplifier and speakers. Because they are connected to the "audio out" of the VCR, they are simply monitoring the audio signal being recorded onto the videotape.

As long as we are referring to audio output, we need to mention audio feedback. Audio feedback is the loud whine/squeal sound that comes from a speaker when a microphone "hears itself." If the audio output of the VCR is to be amplified and played over stereo speakers during a narrated audio dub, the microphone must be placed so that it cannot "hear itself" coming from the speakers. For this application, a cardioid microphone and careful speaker placement are essential. Remember, the feedback will be recorded on the tape just as it is heard during the audio recording.

Audio recording for video production and postproduction requires careful connection of the audio sources and outputs, and attention to the details of correct audio mixer use. With practice and concentration, the audio system can be mastered and the audio will become an essential element in the overall video production.

## Successful Scriptwriting

As professionals can testify, successful scriptwriting is a craft to be studied and developed over time (figure 1.19). However, if you follow these general rules, you can avoid common problems of beginning video projects.

The first sentence tells the story. The listener should be able to get a grasp of the material by listening to your first sentence.

> *Incorrect:*   "The student council had a meeting yesterday."

> *Correct:*   "The student council has decided the theme for this year's homecoming dance."

Keep it short. Simple narration and news items should take only 15-20 seconds.

> *Incorrect:*   "The student council has decided the theme for this year's homecoming. The theme was selected by 41 members of the council. Three members voted against...."

> *Correct:*   "The student council has decided the theme for this year's homecoming. The theme is...."

Fig. 1.19. A student scriptwriting session.

Use active voice; use action verbs.

*Incorrect:*      "The game was won by our baseball team."

*Correct:*        "The baseball team won the game."

Use short words and short sentences.

*Incorrect:*      "The baseball team won the game yesterday, after scoring three runs in the first inning and three more runs in the penultimate inning, anticipating a perennial trip to the district-level tournament, which begins next week.

*Correct:*        "The baseball team won another big game yesterday. The Panthers scored three runs in the first inning and three more in the sixth. The team begins its quest for another district title in next week's tournament.

Don't headline. Every sentence needs a complete, agreeing subject and verb.

*Incorrect:*      "Baseball team crushes Central High."

*Correct:*        "The baseball team crushed Central High yesterday, 6-0."

Use a "people" angle. People like to hear about themselves and other people.

*Incorrect:*      "Three Panthers had two hits each, and another player hit a home run."

*Correct:*        "Scott Mulhan, Tim Bates, and Brian Barber each had two hits. Bobby Hanousek smacked a home run over the left-field wall."

Develop a conversational style. Be "friendly" without sounding frivolous.

*Incorrect:*   "All students who wish to run for the office of student body president should register in room 710 with Mr. Dunlap and prepare to fill out a lengthy application."

*Correct:*   "Have you ever thought about running for student body president? Well, if that sounds exciting, stop by room 710. Mr. Dunlap has the applications."

Give qualifications of names. Don't expect the viewers to know someone just because you do.

*Incorrect:*   "Bill Corrente and John Nadler voted in favor of increased funding to schools."

*Correct:*   "State legislators Bill Corrente and John Nadler voted in favor of increased funding to schools."

Read the story aloud. If the script doesn't make sense to you, it won't make sense to your audience.

*Incorrect:*   "Principal Joann Williams stressed that all grades will be based on class achievement, not the overall achievement of the classwork given to the student in the elective required."

*Correct:*   "Principal Joann Williams stressed that all grades will be based on class achievement, not personal preference of the teacher."

Confirm all facts. If a story sounds too good or bad to be true, it probably is. For example, the following announcement should be confirmed: "Principal Joann Williams announces there will be no school tomorrow!"

## Electronic Character Generation

Electronic character generation is used in almost every type of video production. Documentaries, commercials, and even home movies now include titles, credits, and internal graphics describing the task or content. A few years ago, electronic graphics were solely in the domain of professional television production. But recent developments in electronic and computer technology have made character generation possible for most school video production departments. Three types of character generation are found in schools: camera-based graphics, consumer-oriented graphics, and professional graphics.

*Camera-based graphics* can be created with video cameras and camcorders that have built-in character generators (figure 1.20). These often take the form of a small keyboard installed in the side of the camera. The videographer can simply type the appropriate graphic onto the screen, push a separate button to temporarily erase the graphic, then press the same button again when he or she is ready for the graphic. Some less "friendly" camera-based character generators involve only three or four buttons. The letters are displayed one at a time, "A...B...C..." etc., much like a digital watch. This isn't so bad for titles like "A Bad Cabbage" or "A Cab Ace." But selecting the title "A Buzzing Yellow Zebra" could take all day. Still other cameras/camcorders offer a separate character generator about the size of a hand-held calculator that installs into a specific port on the camera.

Using these camera-based character generators usually involves rolling videotape and recording the graphic, using the viewfinder as a monitor. Most systems record graphics over video footage being recorded simultaneously, as well as graphics over a solid background color. Some offer a choice of character colors, while others offer only black and white. Of course, all of this is rather difficult on a monochrome camera viewfinder. Many school-based video programs use camera-based graphics. However, most schools should consider purchasing a consumer or professional generator after its next fund-raiser or budget allocation.

*Consumer-oriented character generators* offer a middle step for schools that have graduated from camera-based graphics but do not have the finances or need for a professional system. This equipment takes two forms: stand-alone generators and computer programs.

Several companies produce stand-alone consumer-oriented character generators designed to be integrated into home VCRs and camcorders. These generators usually offer a minimum number of type styles, or fonts. Most are able to scroll (bottom to top) and generate a multitude of colors. Because electronic character generators are really small computers with a single program, many schools decide to forego the purchase of a character generator and instead purchase computer software to run on computers that they already own. These programs range from very simple to quite complex, and their features vary as well. While many of these computer-based generators offer near-broadcast quality, they require the exclusive use of a personal computer. If the school has a very limited number of computers designated for student and faculty use, it may be difficult to dedicate a computer to full-time character generation, and the integration of the computer into the video system may be complicated and time-consuming. Exercise caution before purchasing a relatively inexpensive software program to substitute for even the most elementary stand-alone character generator.

*Professional character generators* (figure 1.21) offer all of the features of consumer-oriented generators and rock-solid characters that will endure miles of video cable and several generations of duplication. Professional generator prices start at about $1,000 for the most basic models. Many professional character generators offer memory functions, ranging from 10-15 pages stored in the hardware of the generator using a ni-cad battery to internal floppy and hard-disk drives that can store an infinite number of pages and sequences. Ask about all of the possible uses for the equipment and get a demonstration before purchasing.

Fig. 1.20. Built-in character generator.

## Character Composition

Successful character generation, like scriptwriting, is a craft and an art. The best graphics grab the audience's attention and convey information verbally in a brief time span. If you follow these simple rules, your graphics will communicate effectively to your audience.

- Be aware of character size as it relates to the viewing situation. If you are preparing graphics for broadcast television, you can use smaller sizes than if you are producing a program to be seen in a classroom from a distance of about 20 feet. The graphics for the latter need to be quite large.

Fig. 1.21. Professional character generator.

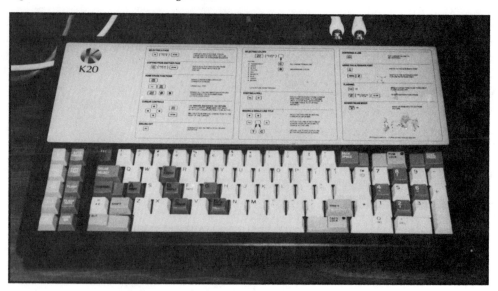

- Use a variety of fonts. If your generator is capable of producing various type sizes, learn to access them and use them in your programs. Your audience will respond favorably to two fonts on a screen (figure 1.22).

Fig. 1.22. Fonts available from a stand-alone character generator.

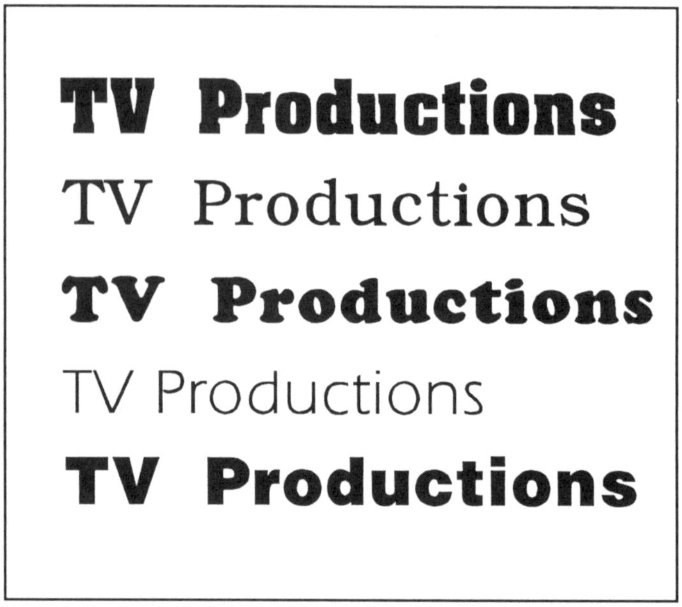

**TV Productions**

TV Productions

**TV Productions**

TV Productions

**TV Productions**

- Use contrasting colors. Go for a high contrast, and avoid pastels that may dissipate when broadcast or duplicated.

- When using a transparent background, be aware of the contrast between the characters and the video footage. White characters may look great on a black background, but when superimposed over a yellow blouse, the white characters are lost.

- Don't overcrowd a page (figure 1.23). Three pages of graphics with two lines each will communicate more effectively than one page with six lines. After two or three lines, your audience will give up. (How many people have actually read the FBI warning on the front of rented video movies?)

**Fig. 1.23. Examples of incorrect and correct character composition.**

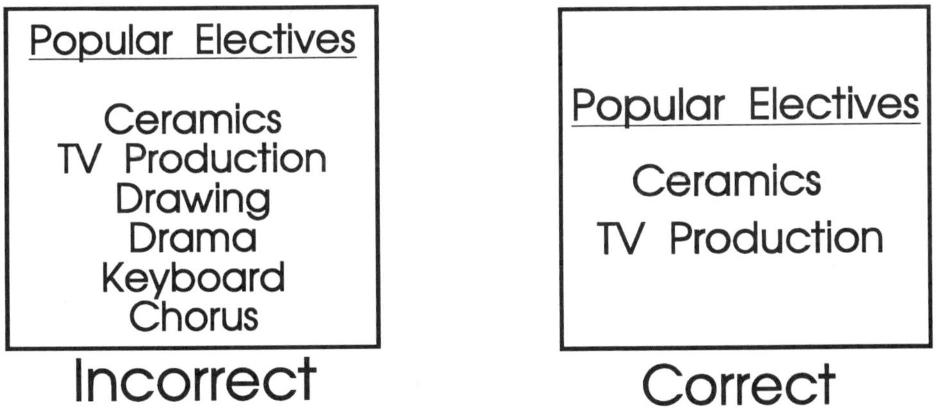

```
┌──────────────────────┐
│  Popular Electives    │
│                       │
│       Ceramics        │
│     TV Production     │
│       Drawing         │
│        Drama          │
│       Keyboard        │
│        Chorus         │
└──────────────────────┘
      Incorrect
```

```
┌──────────────────────┐
│                       │
│  Popular Electives    │
│                       │
│      Ceramics         │
│                       │
│     TV Production     │
│                       │
└──────────────────────┘
       Correct
```

- Keep it simple. Your audience is prepared to watch a program, not read a book. Use characters to accent your video, not replace it.

The use of audio equipment, script, and character generation can certainly add to a video program. Used wisely, these aspects of basic postproduction form the building blocks for the complex video programs that most students want to create and most audiences want to see.

## *Review Questions: Lesson 3*

1. All audio that goes into the videotape recorder should be processed by an _____.

2. A _____ microphone is usually best for an audio dub.

3. The audiocassette input on the audio mixer is usually labeled _____.

4. The compact disc input on the audio mixer console is usually labeled _____.

5. The level of the sound being input into the mixer is controlled by a _____ or a _____.

6. A _____ shows the audio technician the level of the sound entering the audio mixer.

7. If the audio input is correctly adjusted, the VU meter should _____ the red, but not _____.

8. The audio input can be calibrated by adjusting the _____.

9. When a microphone "hears itself," the result is called _____.

10. Using action verbs in scripts is called _____.

11. Every sentence in a script needs a _____ and a _____.

12. In character generation, an attractive screen should contain a variety of _____, or type styles.

13. A good rule for character generation is: "Keep It _____."

# Activities: Lesson 3

1.  Record a few commercials from radio or television and analyze them: Who is the desired audience? What are the strong points and weak points? Does the commercial effectively sell the product or service?

2.  Visit a local television or radio station and ask to see their audio mixer.

3.  While visiting the television station, ask to see the character generator. How does it compare to the character generator that you use in school?

4.  Obtain a news script from a radio or television station. How does it compare to the newspaper article of the same news story?

5.  Ask your teacher to describe the famous Lake Michigan commercial, as cited in the "Notes to the Teacher," page I-1-116. Create a similar commercial.

## *Student Project Plan: Audio Commercial*

### DESCRIPTION OF COMPLETED PROJECT

The completed project will be a 30- to 45-second commercial about a product or service. The audio portion will consist of an announcer reading a script, and appropriate background music. The video will consist of generated graphics, including the announcer's name, class period, the date, the name of the audio technician, and the name of the client (product or service company).

### METHOD

1. Each student will write a script for a 30- to 45-second *audio-only* commercial.

2. Each student will select appropriate background music.

3. Students will practice reading their scripts.

4. On the assigned day, the student will type his or her graphics into the character generator, cue up the music, and prepare to read the script.

5. A volunteer will work as the audio technician.

6. The student will record the commercial on his or her videotape.

### EQUIPMENT

audio mixer

character generator

microphone

music source (tape/CD player, etc.)

VCR

### EVALUATION

The project will be worth 100 points:

| | |
|---|---|
| script | (25) |
| graphics | (25) |
| voice performance | (30) |
| music selection | (20) |

## *Evaluation Sheet: Audio Commercial*

NAME _____

| | | |
|---|---|---|
| Script | (25) | _____ |
| Graphics | (25) | _____ |
| Voice performance | (30) | _____ |
| Music selection | (20) | _____ |
| Total | (100) | _____ |
| Letter grade | | A   B   C   D   Re-do |

**COMMENTS:**

# Lesson 4  Complex ENG Assignments

## Objectives

After successfully completing this lesson, you will be able to:

- *name, recognize, and create the various shots commonly composed in video production.*

- *understand the concepts of headroom, noseroom, and leadroom.*

- *understand the correct use of automatic gain control, automatic iris, white balance, and other camera features.*

- *storyboard the video, audio, and time of a simple video program.*

## Vocabulary

**Automatic gain control.** A camera feature that, when selected, automatically boosts the video signal to an optimal level.

**Automatic iris.** A camera feature that, when selected, automatically adjusts the lens aperture according to the brightest level of the video picture.

**Bust shot.** Video composition that includes the bust area, the head, and a small but comfortable space above the head.

**Close-up.** Video composition that includes the area of the shoulders up to a small distance above the top of the head.

**Extreme close-up.** Video composition that includes all or a portion of the face only.

**Fade button.** A camera operation control that, when used, makes the next press of the trigger a fade to or from a background color, as opposed to a simple tape start or stop.

**Headroom.** The concept of shot composition that dictates a small but comfortable area above the top of the head of the person in the shot.

**Leadroom.** The concept of shot composition that dictates an area in front of a moving object. The camera "leads," rather than centers or follows the activity of the person in the shot.

**Long shot.** Video composition that includes a full body shot of the person in the shot, as well as a moderate area above and below the subject.

**Medium shot.** Video composition that includes the person in the shot down to the waist or knee area including a small but comfortable area above the head.

**Noseroom.** The concept of video composition that dictates a substantial area in front of a person in full or partial profile. Noseroom lets the person in the shot "look" across the screen.

**Over-the-shoulder shot.** Video composition that includes the subject of the shot (animal, vegetable, or mineral) and the shoulder and part of the back of someone's head.

**Remote VCR start button.** A camera operational control button, usually located near the camera thumb-rest, that allows the videographer to roll videotape. The remote VCR start button is commonly known as the trigger.

**Standby.** A camera operational control that, when implemented, deactivates most of the power functions of the camera.

**Storyboarding.** The process of planning a video project that includes drawing a simple sketch of the desired shot, planning the accompanying audio, and estimating the duration of each element in the program.

**White-balance.** The process of adjusting the colors of a video camera that usually includes displaying the color white in front of the camera and pushing a button or series of buttons.

Television has the power to convey information and emotion more than any other medium. That information and emotion is shaped by the electronic news gathering (ENG) videographer. Whether the topic is a political rally, a museum opening, or a natural disaster, the ENG videographer needs to collect the video footage that tells the story. Because the videographer often doesn't get a second chance to get the right shots, knowledge of the video camera and careful planning play an important role in the ENG process. Three important aspects of field shooting—shot selection, camera operational controls, and storyboarding—are featured in this lesson.

## Shot Selection

Although an infinite number of shots can be created with a video camera, certain shots have been established as basic camera angles for television production. These shots are standardized throughout the television industry, so it is important to learn the terminology. By mastering these shots, you will learn the "lingo" of videographers all over the world. Study the photographs and the descriptions, and when a director asks you to line up a medium shot, you'll know exactly what he or she is talking about.

*Long shot (LS).* In a long shot, the subject's (person's) entire body is in the shot (figure 1.24). There is area above the subject's head and below the subject's feet. Combined, the area above the subject and below the subject should be equivalent to the height of the subject; the area above the subject should be twice the size of the area below the subject. Remember, the subject is not always a person. Imagine a long shot of a chair, a house, or a cheeseburger. For this reason, a specific distance from the subject is not specified. A long shot of a cheeseburger might be taken from 2 or 3 feet, while a long shot of a house would be taken from across the street or down the block.

Fig. 1.24. Long shot.

*Medium shot (MS).* A medium shot is harder to define. When the subject is a person, a medium shot is taken from the knees up with a small but comfortable area above the person (figure 1.25). A medium shot of a "nonperson" subject usually fills about 75 percent of the frame.

Fig. 1.25. Medium shot.

*Close-Up (CU).* The close-up is one of the staple shots of video and usually involves a shot of a person. The close-up includes the area of the shoulders up to a small distance above the top of the head (figure 1.26). A close-up of a computer disc would fill the screen with the disc.

**Fig. 1.26. Close-up.**

*Extreme close-up (ECU).* The extreme close-up takes the close-up shot a bit closer. An extreme close-up of a person fills the screen with the face (figure 1.27). Areas such as the top of the head, the base of the chin, or the ears may be eliminated from the extreme close-up. While the ECU probably wouldn't be used by a television reporter, it can be very effective in dramatic or persuasive programs.

**Fig. 1.27. Extreme close-up.**

*Bust shot (BUST).* The bust shot is similar to the medium shot and the close-up. The bust shot includes the bust area while maintaining a comfortable area above the head (figure 1.28). This shot is often used by television reporters because it provides a good picture of the reporter while allowing the viewer to see information behind the reporter or to the side of the reporter.

**Fig. 1.28. Bust shot.**

*Over-the-Shoulder shot.* The over-the-shoulder shot, as the name implies, is taken with the camera "looking over a person's shoulder (figure 1.29). This perspective gives the viewer a sense of participation in the shot and offers the viewer a second angle of the content to avoid boredom. An over-the-shoulder shot is generally a bust shot, but with the shoulder and about half of the back of the head of another person visible. An example would be a reporter interviewing a media specialist

**Fig. 1.29. Over-the-shoulder shot.**

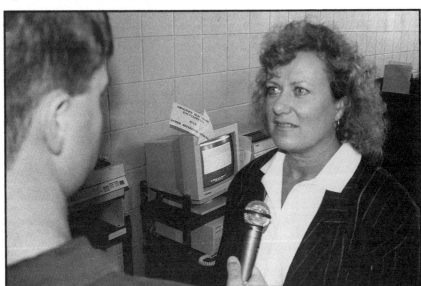

about the new CD-ROM system in the high school, as seen in figure 1.29. The example gives the viewer the perspective of being next to the media specialist as she speaks. In other words, the shot removes the barrier of detachment so often found in television.

Many news reporters are using over-the-shoulder shots for "reaction" shots to insert into lengthy interview sound bites. During an interview with the mayor a reporter asks the question "What can the average person do to help in the recycling effort?" The answer will probably be long, and every word is important. To keep the audience interested, the videographer shoots a few seconds of an over-the-shoulder reaction shot to include in the newscast. The subject in this shot is the reporter, and the shot is taken over the shoulder of the mayor. The reporter nods her head in a response of understanding as the mayor continues to explain the city's recycling effort.

Does the reporter interrupt the mayor during his answer and ask him to continue once the videographer is in place for the over-the-shoulder shot? Or does the station send two videographers to record the interview, one from each perspective? No. The sound bite is recorded exclusively as a bust shot of the mayor. The over-the-shoulder shot is taken after the comment is completed. Sometimes the reporter asks a second question as the videographer records the over-the-shoulder shot. Other times, the reporter simply tells the subject what's happening. Most people who are interviewed on a regular basis know the routine and are glad to help. Of course, during the over-the-shoulder shot, the reporter must not talk (moving lips would not work as an edit) and the subject (in this case, the mayor) must refrain from gestures (such as waving arms) that would seem uncharacteristic for the bust shot. Remember, the mayor's lips are not shown in the over-the-shoulder shot, so the words don't have to be synchronized.

Another use for the over-the-shoulder shot comes when explaining a task for the viewer to learn. Let's say you're making a program for the electronics teacher on how to solder a circuit board. Rather than show two disembodied hands working on the circuit board, you could use a variety of over-the-shoulder shots to give the viewer a size and spatial reference. You can probably think of many other applications for the over-the-shoulder shot in the context of instructional videotape programs.

*Headroom.* While not a shot in itself, the concept of having the proper amount of headroom is important to television production. Headroom refers to the amount of space above the subject's head in the shot. Unfortunately, this concept is difficult to define. Certainly, a videographer wouldn't want to cut off the top of the head on a close-up or bust shot. Learning to avoid "too much" headroom is a more difficult skill to acquire. The tendency for novice videographers is to center the subject's face in the shot. However, as seen in figure 1.30, this gives the effect of a very short reporter. It seems like the subject is standing on his or her toes, peeking into the shot. Draw an imaginary line about one-third of the way down the shot. The eyes should match that imaginary line (figure 1.31). Once again, setting the appropriate headroom takes practice and instruction from an experienced videographer. After the concept of headroom is mastered, aligning the proper shot will become second nature.

Fig. 1.30. Example of too much headroom.

**Fig. 1.31. Example of a proper amount of headroom.**

*Noseroom/Leadroom.* Just as every shot needs a comfortable amount of headroom, every shot in which your subject is walking, running, or just sitting or standing in profile needs a proper amount of noseroom or leadroom. Noseroom is closely related to headroom. When a subject is facing in one direction, during a close-up on a talk show, for example, the shot should not be centered. Instead the camera shot should be about one-third off-center, with the subject given about two-thirds of the screen to look in that direction. This is known as the proper amount of noseroom. Noseroom gives the viewer a stronger sense of direction in close-ups. Let's return to our talk show example. Your class is taping a talk show using two cameras. Camera 1 is a close-up of the host, who is seated on the right. Camera 2 is a close-up of the guest, who is seated on the left. If both camera 1 and camera 2 failed to recognize the noseroom rule, the viewer would have a difficult time distinguishing the placement of the host and the guest on the set. By applying the principal of noseroom, and shooting in a crossing pattern (the camera on the left shooting the close-up on the right and the camera on the right shooting the close-up on the left), the viewers can understand the positioning of the participants and feel that they are in the same room as the guest. Using the proper amount of noseroom gives the subject's eyes space to "see" within the shot and avoids talking lips colliding against the edge of the screen.

When the subject of your video is moving, the principle of noseroom is converted to the term "leadroom." Just as the videographer should leave about a third of the screen empty in front of a stationary subject, he or she should also give the walking or running subject about half of the shot to walk/run toward (figure 1.32). Examples of this rule include football players running down the field, students crossing the stage to receive awards, and surfers chopping through the waves. The scenes described above can be exciting and interesting if shot with the proper amount of leadroom. If we center our football player in the shot as he carries the ball down the field, we have no way of anticipating the bone-jarring tackle he receives from his opponent. With a proper amount of leadroom, the viewer can see the tackle before it happens, adding dramatic effect to the shot. The awards assembly shot is much more exciting if the camera leads, not follows, the student toward her award for being chosen valedictorian. And the thrill of watching the surfing video comes not from seeing the surfer/surfboard centered on the screen, but from seeing the surfer led into the next wave by the expert videographer.

Leadroom and noseroom, just like headroom, are techniques to be practiced and studied. Beginning shots can be analyzed by the student and instructor to learn proper alignment. After mastering the concepts of headroom, noseroom, and leadroom, your shots will be more exciting, involving, and easier for the viewer to understand.

## Camera Operational Controls

Whether you're using a new three-chip professional camera or a slightly used camcorder, your camera probably has a few features that you need to know about. The features discussed in the following paragraphs are found on most cameras/camcorders currently on the market. Learning to correctly use these features will add quality to your video programs.

Fig. 1.32. Example of proper amount of leadroom.

Probably the most important adjustment on your camera is the *white balance.* The white balance adjusts the color response of your camera's imaging device based on the lighting, or "color temperature," of the environment for your shot. A video signal is made of the three primary colors of light—red, blue, and green. These are additive light colors, and different from paint-mixing and still color photography. When all three of the additive colors—red, blue, and green—are present in equal strengths, the result is white light. Therefore, when you white-balance a camera, you are showing the imaging device what the picture should look like when all three colors are being processed at full strength. A simple analogy involves tuning an automobile engine. The mechanic must test the engine at full throttle to assess the car's performance. When you white-balance a camera, you show the camera what video "full-throttle" looks like. The camera then makes electronic adjustments to correspond all colors with the white-balance reading.

Generally, white-balancing a camera involves showing the camera something white—an index card, a white shirt, a white wall—and pushing a button or a series of buttons. The process takes only about five seconds, but the results are critical. Fluorescent lights cast a blue tint onto a shot, changing beautiful blonde hair into a lovely shade of green, and incandescent light gives the entire scene a reddish tinge. Outdoor reflected light can also ruin a shot if the camera is not white-balanced. A person standing in front of a green wall will catch some reflected light from the wall with the result being a greenish complexion. White-balancing on a sheet of typing paper held by the talent can cure the problem.

If at all possible, select a manual white balance over the camera's automatic white-balance settings. Most cameras feature automatic white balancing. Some are equipped with "indoor" or "outdoor" selections. Others offer the choices of "fluorescent" or "incandescent." As you've probably surmised, these settings offer very general choices programmed by a technician many miles away. Also, these settings have a way of deteriorating over time. Tube cameras are more susceptible to deterioration in color than CCD cameras, but CCD cameras have also been known to lose a clear automatic white balance.

Always white-balance your camera immediately before each shot. White-balancing in the classroom will not help the color in the cafeteria. Remember, white-balancing applies to the lighting of the particular environment for the shot. Shots that are not white-balanced should not be used in video production. The distraction of blue faces and green hair far outweighs the content of any scene.

Another common camera feature is *automatic gain control,* or AGC. Lesson 3 indicated that AGC is an audio function that automatically adjusts the sound to an optimum level. On a camera, automatic gain control adjusts the video signal for optimum output in low-light situations. In a general sense, a video AGC is a "power booster" for the video signal. It takes a weak video signal and amplifies it before the VCR records it. As you learned earlier, a camera converts light into a video signal. When the illumination for your videotaping is low, the resulting video signal will be weak. Automatic gain control amplifies that weak signal. Because AGC is an automatic function, the signal will not be amplified unless it is weak. If you turn your AGC button on (or "up"), your camera will amplify weak signals, while leaving strong signals untouched.

There is a disadvantage of using automatic gain control. The amplified weak signal is often "snowy," the slang term for video noise. The weak signal is generally not filtered before it is amplified. In other words, the "noisy" weak signal becomes an even "noisier" strong signal. Sometimes the resulting loss in picture quality outweighs the brightness gained by using AGC.

Most cameras are equipped with *automatic iris controls (auto iris).* The iris is the mechanism within the lens of the camera that controls how much light is let into the camera through the lens. The iris controls the small hole, called the aperture, through which light passes. On a bright, sunny day, the automatic iris contracts to make the aperture very small. Indoors, or at night, the automatic iris opens the aperture to allow the lens to gather all of the available light.

Unlike AGC, auto iris really doesn't have any significant disadvantages. Most cameras use auto iris on a continuing basis. However, all videographers should be aware of the theory behind auto iris: Auto iris is determined by the brightest part of your shot. This can pose a problem. Here's an example: An ENG crew (reporter and videographer) is assigned a news story about the dedication of a new band shell at the city's largest park. For her lead-in, the reporter arrives at noon and stands in the shade of the band shell stage as the videographer shoots toward the now-empty seats. The camera's auto iris keys on the bright noon-time sky, not the reporter's shaded face. The result: A perfect background of the seats and a silhouette of the reporter. Unlike the human eye, the camera cannot adjust to such drastic changes in light. The camera's maximum ratio is about 30:1, meaning the brightest point can only be 30 times brighter than the darkest point. Obviously, our example fails this test. The videographer now has three choices.

- Switch from auto iris to manual iris. Opening the aperture with the iris brightens the reporter's face. Unfortunately, the entire scene becomes lighter, and the background becomes an unintelligible sea of white.

- Use a light to illuminate the reporter. The bright light in broad daylight may draw some inquisitive stares from onlookers, but the result will be a balanced shot that stays within the contrast ratio.

- Change locations.

Choice 2—using the portable light—is the winner here, but because some schools don't have access to this equipment, the other choices may have to suffice. Remember, like the other features in this section, auto iris is a tool of the videographer. If the tool is not needed, it should not be used.

Many cameras have a *standby* setting. Standby eliminates power to most parts of the camera, while maintaining warm-up and white-balance capabilities. The main benefit of standby is power savings. Let's say your ENG assignment is to videotape the President disembarking Air Force One upon arrival in your city. Like any good videographer, you arrive early and position your tripod for good composition. But the President has some last-minute details to attend to, and your battery is running down. Turning the camera "off" would lose the white balance. And most cameras take at least a few seconds to warm up to their optimum performance level. Your solution: Use standby to save your battery power. As the door of the jet opens, take the camera off standby. The white balance has been saved, and no warm-up time is required. Roll tape.

Because ENG camera operators have to be ready at a moment's notice, most cameras are equipped with a *remote VCR start button*, called a *trigger* in production lingo (figure 1.33). The camera trigger is usually located near the thumb rest of the video camera. By using this trigger, the videographer can start and stop (or pause and un-pause) the videotape recorder. This convenient feature is frequently used by videographers.

Fig. 1.33. Trigger.

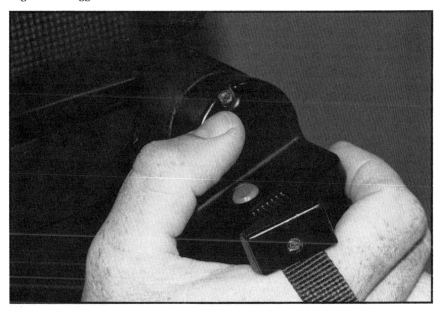

A variation of the trigger is the *fade button.* The fade button allows the videographer to fade out of a shot, rather than have the shot end abruptly. Some cameras fade to black; others to white. Some give a choice.

Another variation of the trigger is the *record review* button. Record review, like the trigger, allows the videographer to control the videotape recorded from the camera. In record review, the VCR switches to "play," searches back about three seconds, plays the last two seconds of video recorded on the tape through the camera viewfinder, and then returns the camera to "record." In other words, record review allows the videographer to see the last few seconds of video made. Perhaps you noticed a time discrepancy in the explanation above; the VCR rewinds three seconds but plays only two. This is your insurance policy to prevent blank tape—a glitch—on your recorded video program. So each time you use record review, you lose about a second of video program. It is possible, then, to cut off an important part of your program by using record review to watch the shot over and over again, and then record another scene on the tape.

Two videotape recorder functions deserve mentioning, as their improper use can sabotage a video production. The VCR *tracking* control aligns the video signal on the tape and should always be adjusted to midpoint when recording. *Tape speed* should always be set at the fastest speed on VHS/S-VHS videotape recorders and camcorders. The fastest speed is known as SP, for "standard play." Other speeds include a speed twice as slow (EP or LP) and one three times as slow (SLP). As you have probably guessed, a faster tape speed gives a better-quality video picture, and most higher-quality videocassette decks can only play on the fastest speed. The only proper use for a slower speed is if an event that you are recording lasts longer than expected and you have to switch speeds midway through the program. In the 1970s, VHS videotape was very expensive—$15-$20 per tape. Because it was strictly for home use (*Video Home System*) it made sense to record 6 hours instead of 2 hours onto a videocassette. Now, with VHS as a viable format for schools and other closed-circuit applications, and the price of excellent-quality videotape in the $5 price range, the quality given from recording at the fastest speed far outweighs any tape cost. To unnecessarily record on a slower speed is foolish and detrimental to the video production.

## Storyboarding

Storyboarding is the process of planning a video production by drawing a simple sketch of the desired video shot, writing the audio portion (or description of the audio), and listing an approximate time for the sequence. Storyboarding is a very important part of the production process. By sketching each individual shot in a format such as that shown in figure 1.34, the production team can create the video project on paper before making costly and time-consuming mistakes on camera. Most video producers can relate stories of the times they thought storyboarding really wasn't necessary for a simple shoot, only to realize during the editing process that a crucial shot had been forgotten.

Storyboard creation is a skill that improves with practice and experience. If you follow these simple pieces of advice, your early storyboarding attempts will be successful.

1.  Keep it simple. Even if you're an aspiring artist, stick to simple drawings. Remember, storyboards serve to remind the producers of the composition of the shots. Minor details aren't important.

2.  Draw the actual shot. Beginning storyboarders often leave too much headroom in storyboards. Imagine watching the video program on your television, and draw the shot you wish to create (figure 1.35, page I-1-56). If you want a close-up, draw a close-up. Sometimes it helps to close your eyes for a few seconds to visualize the shot before drawing.

3.  Consider point of view. Let's say you are planning to videotape a dialogue from a play for your English teacher. You could record the entire scene as a two-shot medium shot, but it would be much more interesting to record some lines from the audience's point of view, some from the first character's point of view, and still others from the second character's point of view. Storyboarding the different points of view can make the final program more interesting to watch.

4.  Use the margins for notes. List whether the shot is a long shot, a medium shot, etc. This gives the videographer more information with which to work and can compensate for less talented storyboard artists.

5.  Use arrows to indicate panning and camera movement. Remember, the storyboards are your notes. Make notes under the sketches or in the margins. If your opening shot requires the narrator to walk into a medium shot from out of camera range, draw the narrator in the medium shot and draw an arrow pointing from off-camera to the back of the narrator. In the margins, write "talent walks into frame, medium shot." The same technique can be used for pans and zooms.

6.  Make a rough estimate of the length of the shot and list that time on the storyboard. If you are editing, make sure to roll the tape at least five seconds before action starts and leave it rolling for about five or ten more seconds after the action concludes. If you are not editing, remember that most videotape recorders require one or two seconds to begin recording on the tape after the trigger is pushed. If your talent begins to speak the moment the trigger is pushed, the first few words will not be recorded.

(Text continues on page I-1-56.)

Fig. 1.34. Storyboard.

Program _____ Page _____ of ___

Producers _____

| VISUAL | TIME | AUDIO |
|--------|------|-------|

Fig. 1.35. Storyboard.

Actual Shot

*Close-up*

*Working on Ceramics*

7. Don't forget to storyboard the audio. If your script is already written, list the first few words of the script for each shot. If your script has not been written, make a note of the content to be covered in the audio. Also, note in the audio section whether the sound is "live" sound (to be recorded at the same time as the video) or a "voice-over," to be audio-dubbed at a later time.

   Music is also selected during the storyboarding process. Good background music is integrated into the program, not just added to pass time between narration segments. If you haven't selected the exact piece of music, list the type of music, for example, "light and breezy," "tough/action music," or "scary music."

Students will invariably ask, "Do I have to storyboard *every* shot?" The answer is an emphatic YES! A local high school video team storyboarded 21 shots for a 1-minute action sequence in which a coward confronted the neighborhood bully. Without such careful planning, such a complex sequence could not have been completed.

Careful storyboarding, knowledge of the different camera angles used in video, and knowledge of the special features of your video camera can make your videos more informative and entertaining.

# *Review Questions: Lesson 4*

1. What is the difference between noseroom and leadroom?

2. Why is it important to white-balance a camera?

3. What are the three primary colors of light used in television production?

4. How does fluorescent light affect the color processed by a video camera?

5. What are two problems with using automatic white balance?

6. Where and when should white balancing take place?

7. Under what conditions should automatic gain control be used?

8. What is the main disadvantage of using AGC?

(Review questions continue on page I-1-58.)

9. List three ways to shoot a scene that surpasses the 30:1 contrast ratio.

10. What is the main benefit of the "standby" control?

11. What function does the "trigger" perform?

12. List the main problem with abuse of a "record review" function.

13. Which speed should be used for S-VHS and VHS recording?

14. Why is storyboarding important?

15. List the seven rules of storyboarding.

# *Activities: Lesson 4*

1. Locate the following buttons on a video camera/deck or camcorder that you use at school: automatic gain control, automatic iris control, white balance, standby, trigger, fade, tape speed, tracking.

2. List the other features available on the camera you used above.

3. Videotape examples of close-ups using the proper amount of headroom, too much headroom, and too little headroom. Do the same with noseroom. View the samples in class and evaluate your performance.

4. Obtain three slide mounts and three slide projectors from your school media specialist. Mount a red gel in one slide mount, a blue gel in the second, and a green gel in the third. Using the three slide projectors, project each slide onto the same screen. What do you expect will happen? What really happens? Which principle of video production does this illustrate? (Important note: Make sure to use professional-quality gel, which looks like tinted transparency material but can actually withstand the heat produced by the slide projector. Using regular tinted plastic will cause damage to the projector. Because you only need a few square inches of each gel, your local vendor may donate a sample.)

5. Connect your camera/camcorder to a television or monitor. Using your manual white-balance control, white-balance your camera on a *red* piece of paper. Try blue and green also. What are the results? How do extremely bright colors differ from dull colors?

6. Connect your camera/camcorder to a television or monitor. Darken your classroom so that your camera has the minimum illumination for processing the video signal. Analyze the picture quality. In what ways does the quality suffer? Then, switch to automatic gain control. How does that affect the shot?

7. Create a simple storyboard of at least three different shots for the following three videotaping opportunities:

   a high school football game

   a dance recital

   an automobile dealership commercial

# *Student Project Plan: Documentary*

## DESCRIPTION OF COMPLETED PROJECT

The finished project will be a 3-minute documentary on some facet of life at school. It *may* include an interview. The documentary must contain various camera shots and must contain voice and music audio dub. Titles will be at the beginning, featuring the name of the program and the name of the producers. The last shot will fade to black.

## METHOD

1. Students will choose a partner.
2. The team agrees on a topic.
3. The team creates a set of storyboards for the project. Pre-planning is important. There will be no editing.
4. Students use the character generator to compose a title.
5. Students then shoot the documentary in order.
6. Students audio-dub the documentary with voice and music.

## EQUIPMENT

audio mixer

camera/deck or camcorder

character generator

microphone

music source

tripod (optional)

VCR

## EVALUATION

The project will be worth 200 points:

| | |
|---|---|
| concept and storyboard | (40) |
| titles | (40) |
| camera work | (40) |
| audio dub | (40) |
| overall production | (40) |

# Evaluation Sheet: Documentary

TEAM MEMBERS _____

### Concept and Storyboard

| | | |
|---|---|---|
| Project idea | (10) | _____ |
| Storyboard video | (10) | _____ |
| Storyboard audio | (10) | _____ |
| Completion of idea | (10) | _____ |

### Audio Dub

| | | |
|---|---|---|
| Script | (10) | _____ |
| Music choice | (10) | _____ |
| Mixing levels | (10) | _____ |
| Voice talent | (10) | _____ |

### Titles

| | | |
|---|---|---|
| Choice of title | (10) | _____ |
| Spelling | (10) | _____ |
| Layout | (10) | _____ |
| Choice of colors | (10) | _____ |

### Camera Work

| | | |
|---|---|---|
| Shot selection | (10) | _____ |
| Steadiness | (10) | _____ |
| White balance | (10) | _____ |
| Shot variety | (10) | _____ |

### Overall Production

| | | |
|---|---|---|
| Is the viewer more informed on the topic area? | (20) | _____ |
| Is the project free from serious production problems? | (10) | _____ |
| Is the treatment of the topic fresh, creative, and thought-provoking? | (10) | _____ |

COMMENTS:

Total Points/Percentage _____ / _____ %

Letter grade      A    B    C    D    Re-do

# Lesson 5   Single-Camera Studio Production

## Objectives

After successfully completing this lesson, you will be able to:

- *identify and describe the connectors used in video production.*

- *explain the function and use of adapters in video production.*

- *explain the difference between shielded and unshielded cable and understand the proper application for each type.*

- *arrange ENG equipment into a ministudio.*

- *understand concepts of basic set design for a small studio news show.*

- *understand and apply the basic structure of small studio lighting.*

## Vocabulary

**1/4-inch phone.** A type of plug or jack used in audio connections.

**1/8-inch mini.** A type of plug or jack used in audio connections.

**Adapter.** A small connector that allows conversion from one type of jack or plug to another type.

**Backlight.** A light used in television production positioned behind the talent and designed to eliminate the shadow caused by the key light.

**BNC.** A popular twist-lock connector used in video production.

**F connector.** A jack/plug used to connect VCRs to television sets. Also called an RF connector.

**Fill light.** A third light used in small studio video production. It is designed to fill shadow areas caused by the use of a key light.

**Jack.** A receptacle for an audio or video connection.

**Key light.** The main source of artificial illumination in a video production. The key light is usually facing the on-air talent.

**Line-out monitor.** The video or audio/video monitor that displays the final signal produced by the audio/video system.

**Phono.** A type of connector used in audio and video production. Also called an RCA connector.

**Plug.** The part of the connector that is inserted into the jack.

**Shielded cable.** An insulated cable used in audio and video production.

**Unshielded cable.** A cable with little or no insulation used as a stereo speaker cable and headphone cable.

**XLR.** An audio connector usually used with low-impedance, professional systems.

Schools across the nation are using simple television studios within their schools to create shows that entertain and inform their student body, faculty, and administration. Some schools produce daily news shows that replace the standard morning announcements. Other schools choose a weekly or semimonthly schedule in which documentary and feature programs replace timely news items. Whatever the time frame, the news shows provide a source of information as well as a creative and educational outlet for the students involved.

While some schools have studios that cost half a million dollars and more, a news show can be produced with a minimum amount of equipment. In this lesson, we look at the connections needed to assemble your ENG equipment into a small studio and how to design and light your studio for your program needs.

Audio and video equipment can be configured so that it can work together in more complex programs. As you can imagine, the equipment is connected with a series of wires. Fortunately, the connections do not involve removing the external housing of the equipment and installing new wires. Most items of equipment used in audio and video production have various inputs and outputs used to make these connections.

A receptacle for a wire is called a *jack.* The connector that is inserted into the jack is called a *plug.* There are many different jacks and plugs used in audio/video production. While the industry has no formal standard jack/plug type, some are emerging as prominent connection points on audio/video equipment. Still, it is important to learn the proper name and use of each jack/plug that may be encountered in video production. Because smaller school-based programs often use a hodgepodge of ENG and secondhand equipment, students will likely use many of the different jacks/plugs available.

## Connectors Used in Audio

Most audio jacks/plugs are designed for simple connection and disconnection. The main jacks/plugs found in audio production are 1/4-inch phone, 1/8-inch mini, phono (RCA), and XLR.

As can be seen in figure 1.36, the *1/4-inch phone* plug is characterized by a broad metal shaft with an indentation near the end that connects to a plain jack. The 1/4-inch phone plug gets its name from its diameter and its early use by switchboard operators. Now the 1/4-inch phone plug is used for microphone and headphone connections.

The *1/8-inch mini* plug is identical to the 1/4-inch phone plug, except it is about half the size (figure 1.37). The 1/8-inch mini plug was created to accommodate the personal, pocket-sized electronics market. The 1/8-inch mini plug still hasn't made a big dent in studio audio equipment, although its use is increasing in lavaliere microphones and smaller headphone sets.

Music sources are usually connected to an audio mixer via *phono* plugs, commonly referred to as *RCA* plugs, after the company that created and popularized the plug-in home stereo systems. As shown in figure 1.38, the phono plug is a metal shaft that is surrounded by metal flanges that serve to secure the connection. The phone jack is a plain receptacle that is raised from the equipment surface. Phone plugs are popular because of the stereo sound demands of most modern audio equipment. Phone plugs are usually found in pairs: one for the right audio channel and another for the left.

(Text continues on page I-1-65.)

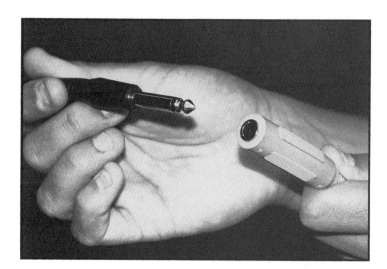

Fig. 1.36. 1/4-inch phone plug.

Fig. 1.37. 1/8-inch mini plug.

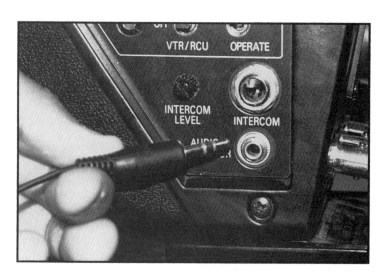

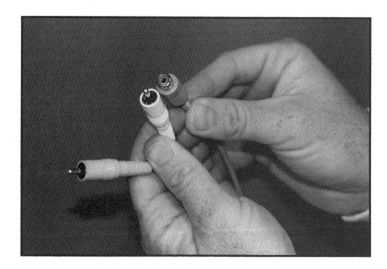

Fig. 1.38. Phono, or RCA, plugs.

They are often colored red and white to avoid confusion when true stereo sound is a goal of the program. (Unfortunately, most school-based television sets are mono, so any channel separation achieved in the studio is often lost on your audience.) Because of the nature of the connection, phono jacks and plugs should be checked on a regular basis for security and firmness. When the audio is not working properly in your system, a loose phono plug is the best place to begin trouble-shooting.

Professional audio systems often use the *XLR* plug/jack system. The XLR plug has three separate plugs encased within a cone-shaped cover (figure 1.39). The XLR jack is simply a unit containing three separate coordinating jacks. XLR plugs/jacks are frequently found in professional TV studios and audio mixers. XLR jacks/plugs are usually used in low-impedance microphone systems using long cable lengths. Often, audio mixers that have XLR jacks also offer the 1/4-inch jack option.

**Fig. 1.39. XLR plugs.**

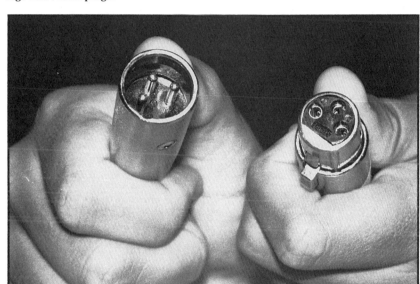

## Connectors Used in Video

Video components must be properly connected to work together in the video production. Unlike audio connectors, connectors used in video offer a more permanent installation. The connectors most often associated with video are RF (or F connector) and BNC.

By far, the most common connector used in video is the *BNC* jack/plug (figure 1.40). The BNC is unique in its twist-lock connection. The BNC plug consists of a small post surrounded by a locking assembly that aligns with the jack and twists into place. This locking mechanism guarantees that the cable will not be disturbed by simple jarring or shaking. The connector is large enough to be strong and easily manipulated and small enough to be space-efficient. In an area once crowded with options, the BNC has emerged as the industry standard.

The *RF*, or *F connector* is used to connect VCRs to television sets (figure 1.41). The RF connector is usually considered a permanent installation because it requires several turns of the screw-on post.

RCA/phono connectors are also used in consumer-grade video.

Fig. 1.40. BNC jack/plug.

Fig. 1.41. RF, or F, connector.

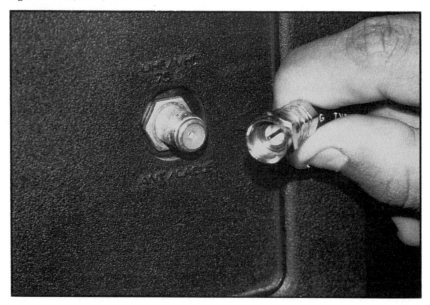

## Adapters

Most electronic stores stock a wide variety of adapters that can convert one type of plug or jack to another. For example, an adapter can be used to convert the 1/8-inch mini plug that is on the end of your lavaliere microphone to the 1/4-inch phone plug that your audio mixer accepts. In many cases, like the one mentioned above, using an adapter is the only option other than cutting the original plug and installing a new one. Sometimes the adapter can also cut costs. Schools wired for closed-circuit television frequently have cable with RF plugs on each end left over from the wall-tap to television connections. These cords can be fitted with adapters that convert them to BNC or RCA for use in the television studio. Many schools also maintain a small supply of adapters for use in unexpected circumstances. A tackle box can be used to keep the adapters in order. Older equipment can also be rendered useful, thanks to adapters. One school recently obtained two high-quality monochrome monitors for a very reasonable price but found the connectors to be quite foreign. A visit to the electronics store garnered two adapters that made the monitors fully functional in the television studio. Many years ago, as video technology was emerging, each company that manufactured video equipment used its own connection system, thus you may encounter some obscure connectors. Once again, a trip to your local electronics dealer will probably solve any problems that you encounter.

## Shielded and Unshielded Cable

Cable that has been insulated (wrapped) in rubber, foam, or both is called shielded cable. Shielded cable should be used in all audio and video connections. The extra insulation maintains signal strength and keeps out interference from such sources as televisions, computers, and fluorescent lights. Unshielded cable, which is generally just copper wire wrapped in plastic, can be used for connecting speakers or headphones to a system—in other words, audio outputs not to be used again by the system. For example, let's say that your microphone cable is not long enough for a needed application. When you visit the electronics store, you find two cables that are similar in appearance and seem to fulfill your need: shielded microphone extension cable and headphone extension cable. The headphone extension cable is less expensive, but it will not serve as a microphone extension cable. Many manufacturers use gray cable to indicate shielded cable and other colors to indicate unshielded cable, but this is far from being an industrywide practice. The correct information can be obtained from the package label, small writing on the cable, or a query of the salesperson. In order to maintain the integrity of your production and the health of your pocketbook, the correct information should be obtained before buying the cable.

## Preparation for System Configuration

Now that you know all about audio and video connectors, you are ready to configure your system into a working studio. Our objective is to produce a single-camera news show with music and voice. Depending on the amount of equipment that you have, you may want to add or delete components.

One concept remains constant in all video connections: the concept of inputs and outputs. Each item of equipment, audio or video, serves to process the signal created by sources—microphones, cameras, and music sources. The input takes in the signal, and the output sends it to the next input. If this concept is cloudy to you, it will become clearer as we continue.

## Audio System Connections

Audio inputs for a small studio consist of microphones and music (music intro and conclusion). If you plan to include an ENG segment that has been prerecorded (e.g., an interview with the principal, a story about the first dance of the school year) you will need audio from a VCR (figure 1.42).

Your anchorperson, or talent, can use a lavaliere microphone or a hand-held microphone on a desktop stand. This microphone should be connected to the audio mixer. If you have more than one anchorperson, each should have his or her own microphone. Sharing or passing around microphones can be noisy and lead to loss of sound quality.

If you plan to use music as your show begins and concludes, you need to connect your music source (cassette/CD player) to the audio mixer, too. If you have chosen to use an ENG segment in your news show, you need to connect the segment's audio to the audio mixer as well. (Playing an ENG segment requires a separate VCR.) Run a shielded cable (or pair for stereo) from the "audio-out" of

Fig. 1.42. Audio connections.

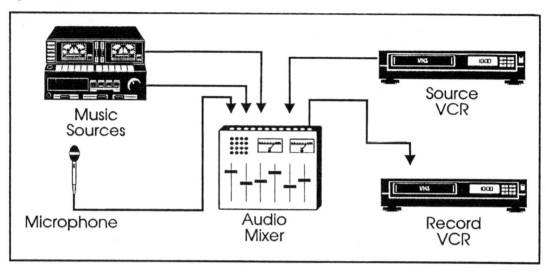

your "play" VCR to an input of your audio mixer. Treat this input as you would a music source, such as an audiotape or CD. Use a pair of headphones so that your audio technician can hear the microphone(s), ENG sound and music, and obtain a proper audio mix.

The audio mixer should have a "main output" set of jacks on the back. Run a shielded cable—or a pair of shielded cables if you are using a stereo-mixing console and VCR—to the audio input jack(s) of your recording VCR. For all practical purposes, your audio connections are complete. If you want other class members to hear the show over stereo speakers as it is being videotaped, you will need a small amplifier and one or two speakers. Run a shielded cable from the audio output of the recording VCR to the tape input of the audio amplifier. Then connect a speaker to the regular speaker output of the audio amplifier.

## Video System Connections

The video portion of our small studio setup consists of a camera or camcorder, a switcher, a character generator, a source VCR for playing segments, and a record VCR for recording the final program (figure 1.43). A simpler configuration is available for schools that don't have a switcher and/or character generator, and will be explained on page I-1-69.

A video switcher is similar in function to an audio mixer. A video switcher selects and combines video sources. For our ministudio, we need a switcher that has at least two video inputs and a background color. The video camera/camcorder is connected to an input of the video switcher. In either case, no VCR is used at the site of the camera. Video cameras and camcorders have video outputs. On camcorders, this might involve searching through the accessory pack for an adapter. If you plan to run an ENG segment during your news show, you need to run a shielded cable from the "video-out" of the "play/segment" VCR to another input of your switcher. Now you have both video sources—camera and source VCR—connected to your switcher. Depending on the type of switcher you have, you may be able to make dissolves, wipes, cuts, etc. Your switcher will also probably offer the option of a monitor so that you can preview a video source before selecting it.

Your next connection adds graphics, such as the name of the anchorperson and ending credits. A shielded cable should connect the "video-out" of the switcher to the "video-in" of the character generator. The output of the character generator is connected to the input of the record VCR. By using the "transparent" background color choice on the character generator, the video signal from the switcher will simply "play through" the character generator as the graphics technician adds the titles,

Fig. 1.43. Video connections.

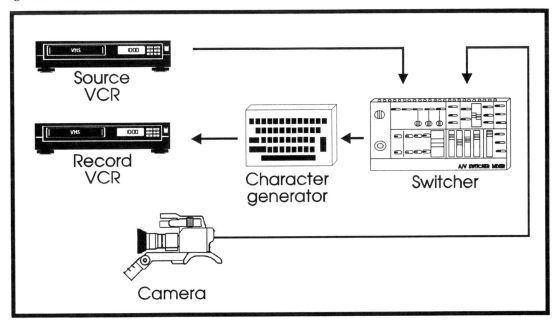

internal graphics, and credits. Most character generators also have "preview out" jacks that can be connected to another monitor to allow the graphics technician to create, select, and preview graphics before they are put on the screen.

Now all audio and video have been connected to the record VCR. Running a shielded cable from the RF out of the record VCR to a television set allows the producer to see and hear the end product. This television is called the line-out monitor.

Let's briefly review the connections explained in the previous paragraphs and also illustrated in figure 1.44. For audio: All sources (microphone/music/source VCR) are connected to the audio mixer. The combined audio signal goes from the audio mixer to the record VCR, where it is recorded simultaneously with the video. For video: Video inputs (camera/source VCR) are connected to a video switcher. The signal is then sent to a character generator for graphics, and then to the record VCR, to be recorded simultaneously with the audio. To see the finished product as it is being recorded, a line-out monitor is connected to the RF out of the record VCR.

*But what if we don't have* an audio mixer, a switcher, or a character generator? Connect a microphone to your camcorder and go on with the show. If you want to use ENG segments, use the deck-to-deck editing techniques described in lesson 6. For music, use a stereo with a speaker near the anchorperson. Use camera-based graphics. But don't stop production. Make video yearbooks, sell candy, write grants, beg your administration. Spend your well-earned funds on the equipment listed above. But continue to produce your news program.

## Basic Set Design

Converting a classroom to a news studio can tax your creativity. Use the following tips to get the job done.

- Keep it simple. A small table with a student or secretary's chair will suffice. Don't distract your viewers with unnecessary items.

- Keep it small. An actual news set can fit in the corner of a classroom. Worry only about what the camera "sees."

Fig. 1.44. Audio and video connections.

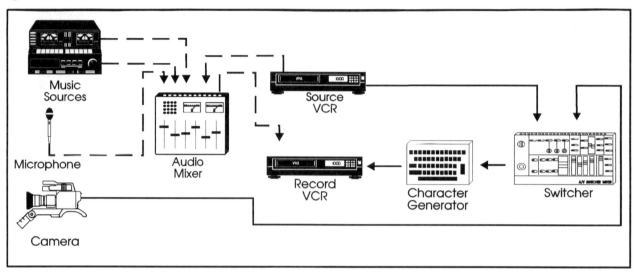

- Seat your anchorperson on a platform. School shop classes might help to construct a wood platform about 4 inches tall. The platform can be 5 to 6 feet long and 4 to 5 feet wide. This platform will allow normal camera operation while eliminating a downward tilt of the camera.

- Use a background. Choose a neutral color like light blue, gray, or tan. Try to use your school colors. Backgrounds can be made of curtains, bulletin board paper, or painted or dyed material. Even ironed bedsheets can be hung on the wall.

- Eliminate empty spots. Fill the screen with your anchorperson and perhaps a simple unobtrusive decoration.

- Constantly think of ways to improve the set. You can probably come up with ideas to improve a basic news set. Use items from around your school to liven up the set.

## Simple Studio Lighting

Although your camera or camcorder can operate effectively under classroom lighting, your picture will probably improve with additional lighting. Professional lighting kits are expensive, but many schools have obtained near-professional results using less-than-professional equipment. Perhaps your drama department has an extra light that can be mounted on the wall or on a tripod. Hardware stores sell inexpensive clamp lights, which consist of a regular bulb socket connected to a reflector dish and a clamp. School maintenance departments can help with floodlight fixtures. (A note of warning: All lights mentioned above produce heat. Don't let your creative lighting designs become a fire hazard! Always verify the safety of your connections with the appropriate authorities.)

If you decide to use lighting in your news program, you will probably need at least two lighting instruments: a main key light and a backlight. The key light's job is to illuminate your anchorperson. The backlight is placed behind the anchorperson near ground level and is pointed up and slightly toward the background. This light will help decrease the shadow caused by the key light. If the backlight does not control the shadow, a third fill light may be used from one side pointed at the anchorperson. Work with your lighting until you have produced a safe, aesthetic design.

A classroom can be converted into a small, working studio with a minimal amount of equipment, the knowledge presented in this lesson, and the creativity to work around program limitations. Producing a school news show can be a rewarding experience!

Have fun!

# *Review Questions: Lesson 5*

1. What is the difference between a jack and a plug?

2. Several connectors are listed below. To the left of each connector, indicate whether its use is primarily in audio or video.

   _____  1/4-inch phone      _____  BNC

   _____  XLR                 _____  phono

   _____  F connector         _____  1/8-inch mini

3. Which type of connector is usually found in pairs?

   Which type of connector is found in professional audio systems?

   Which type of connector uses a twist-lock mechanism?

   Which type of connector is used to connect VCRs to television sets?

4. Video connections are usually [more/less] secure than audio connections. (Circle one.)

5. What is the difference between shielded and unshielded cable?

6. Which type of cable should be used in most audio and video applications?

(Review questions continue on page I-1-72.)

7.   How can a person determine if a cable is shielded or unshielded before purchase?

8.   Why is a line-out monitor important to small studio productions?

9.   List the six tips given for small studio set design.

10.   How can a small studio be illuminated with nonprofessional lights?

11.   What is the top consideration for lighting?

## *Activities: Lesson 5*

1.  Inspect all of your audio and video equipment. Make a list of all of the connectors used. Are they all found in this lesson? Identify any connectors that are new to you.

2.  Identify the connectors used in your home VCR, small electronics, video games, etc. Are they the same as the connectors used in audio and video?

3.  Find the names of connectors used in computer equipment.

4.  Research the meanings behind the abbreviations BNC, RF, RCA, and XLR.

5.  Using a small scale from the science department, weigh equal lengths of shielded and unshielded cable. How do they compare?

6.  Visit a local electronics shop. Ask to see all of the connectors and adapters. Bring a catalog back to the class.

7.  Make a checklist of all of the equipment mentioned in this lesson. Which items does your school have? Which ones should it consider purchasing?

8.  Brainstorm a list of 10 stories that would be interesting for a news show at your school.

9.  Make a simple sketch of a news show set design. Make sure to list all of the materials needed. Be realistic.

# *Student Project Plan: News Brief*

## DESCRIPTION OF COMPLETED PROJECT

The completed project will be a self-contained news program lasting about three minutes. The project will include opening and ending credits with music, a story read on camera by the anchorperson, a videotape story narrated by the anchorperson, and a complete news segment on videotape. The anchor will introduce all segments.

## METHOD

1. Students will choose groups based on jobs and interests.
2. Job descriptions appear on the student handout (see page I-1-75).
3. Titles and assignments are completed.
4. Project is completed using small studio equipment.

## EQUIPMENT

audio mixer

camera/camcorder

character generator

lighting (optional)

line-out monitor

microphone

monitors

music sources

switcher

tripod

two VCRs

## EVALUATION

The project will be worth 200 points. The group will be given a grade of 100 possible points for professional appearance of the production, coordination, and quality of content. Each group member will also be given a possible 100-point grade based on his or her individual work.

# *News Brief Handout*

## FORMAT

| Time | Program | Video Source | Audio Source |
|------|---------|--------------|--------------|
| | | fade from black | |
| :05 | opening | graphics | music |
| :20 | story #1 | camera/graphics | anchor |
| :30 | story #2 | source VCR | anchor |
| 1:00 | story #3 | source VCR | VCR |
| :10 | goodbye | camera | anchor |
| :20 | credits | graphics | music |

## PERSONNEL

Each student is assigned specific tasks to complete before (preproduction) and during (production) the actual program.

*Student #1*   Preproduction: assignment editor, anchor script, lead-ins.

Production: studio anchor

*Student #2*   Preproduction: learn switching skills

Production: switcher, VCR operator

*Student #3*   Preproduction: ENG reporter (story #3)

Production: audio technician

*Student #4*   Preproduction: ENG videographer

Production: videographer/camera setup

*Student #5*   Preproduction: character generator design, ENG assistant

Production: character generator

## *Evaluation Sheet: News Brief*

SHOW TITLE _____

PERIOD _____

|  | Individual Grade | + | Group Grade | = | Total Grade |
|---|---|---|---|---|---|
| Student –1 _____ | _____ | | _____ | | _____ |
| Comments: | | | | | |
| Student –2 _____ | _____ | | _____ | | _____ |
| Comments: | | | | | |
| Student –3 _____ | _____ | | _____ | | _____ |
| Comments: | | | | | |
| Student –4 _____ | _____ | | _____ | | _____ |
| Comments: | | | | | |
| Student –5 _____ | _____ | | _____ | | _____ |
| Comments: | | | | | |

Group's comments:

# Lesson 6 Instructional Techniques for Video

## Objectives

After successfully completing this lesson, you will be able to:

- *select an appropriate topic for an instructional video program.*
- *plan, shoot, edit, and audio-dub an instructional video program.*
- *connect and use a deck-to-deck editing system.*

## Vocabulary

**Black tape.** A videotape onto which a solid black screen and no audio has been recorded. A segment of black tape is used at the beginning and at the end of video programs.

**Continuity.** The practice of detail orientation that makes sure that the video program is consistent from edit to edit.

**Control track.** The part of the recorded videotape that stabilizes the video.

**Deck-to-deck editing.** The process of combining and rearranging videotape segments by connecting two VCRs and duplicating the program in the desired sequence.

**Establishing shot.** In traditional video production, the first segment of a video program that gives the viewer information about the setting. For example, a video program set in a high school would begin with an establishing long shot of the high school exterior.

**Jump cut.** The effect produced when similar video segments with significant differences are juxtaposed in the editing process. For example, the first shot contains a woman sitting on a park bench. In the very next shot, the woman is standing. She has "jumped."

**Live sound.** The audio recorded, using an external microphone or the camera's internal microphone, simultaneously with the video on the videotape. Live sound can be "talent" (someone speaking, singing, or playing a musical instrument) or "ambient" (a naturally existing environmental sound, such as birds singing or waves crashing at the ocean).

**Raw footage.** The video and audio recorded on the videotape during the shoot. The raw footage is edited to make the video program.

Schools, companies, and organizations around the world are using video to instruct people on a wide variety of subjects. Video is an effective medium for communicating the objectives designed by instructors of many tasks. Since the early days of video technology, class and study sessions have been recorded for people to view at other times and places. Those early efforts usually involved setting a camera on a tripod in the back of a classroom and conducting the class session as normal. Or the entire class was brought into the television studio to accommodate the space and lighting needed by early television cameras. But with the advent of video editing, graphics, and ENG equipment, instructional video took a different form. Instructional programs establish the video viewer as the primary audience of the program, not just as a distant observer.

Today, video is a valuable tool for many institutions. Companies regularly produce instructional video programs to train workers on established procedures, announce new procedures, and conduct informative "video meetings." Schools produce video programs to facilitate distance learning and give special tutoring to students having difficulty with certain topics. Through video technology, people can be trained firsthand by experts otherwise not available. The addition of music and professional narration makes the program even more effective.

## Topics for Instructional Videos

Some topics lend themselves naturally to instructional video programs. Video's strongest feature is its ability to convey motion to the viewer. Topics that deal with important behaviors, such as "How to Load a Computer Program" or "How to Make a Fast-Food Sandwich," would make good instructional videos. However, video's strength can also work as a weakness. Topics that require exact, tedious tasks don't translate very well on video, unless still-video technology is used. A video on "How to Connect a Fuse Box" could lead to disaster and might be better suited for a slide show, book, or person-to-person session.

An instructional video must also fit the level of the viewer. A simple rule to follow is to make a "you can" video, not an "I can" video. Instructional video producers should carefully evaluate the current level of expertise of their viewing audience before selecting a topic. For example, a 5-minute video program on "How to Choreograph a Ballet" probably wouldn't work; a 10-minute program on three of the basic ballet positions would be more effective. Remember, tell your audience "you can," not "I can."

For reasons alluded to above, concrete, objective tasks work better as video topics than abstract, subjective topics. "How to Be a Friend" might sound like a great idea for a video program, but the topic is really too personal to communicate real content. "How to Plan a Surprise Party" would capture the same spirit and teach a real skill.

Make sure your instructional programs have real instructions, not just tips. While helpful hints are important, they shouldn't be the entire content of the video.

A topic for an instructional video should be narrow in scope to allow completion of a single skill while achieving some sense of closure. In other words, the viewer should learn to perform a single, complete task. (A single video program on the techniques for video production would be too long and thus ineffective.) After learning more than a few new skills, most viewers suffer from "information overload," that feeling that you have at the end of a class when it seems like your brain just can't hold anymore! Instructional video programs on topics like television production, cooking, or auto repair are usually broken into appropriate subject areas and presented as a series of programs lasting a few minutes each. These programs can be selected for appropriateness and reviewed by the learner as the need arises.

Remember: Not all topics are suitable for instructional video programs. Topics that show simple, concrete skills that the learner can master after one or two viewings work best in the medium of television.

# The Structure of Instructional Video Programs

Like a good novel or short story, an instructional video program should have a beginning, a middle, and an end.

Many options exist for the beginning of instructional video programs. Let's choose a topic and work through many possible introductions. Imagine that you have been contacted by a local sandwich shop to produce a 10-minute video program on the preparation of its new roast beef sandwich. You could begin with a graphic "How to Prepare a Roast Beef Sandwich" on the screen. This reading activity would surely get your audience involved in the task. Perhaps an announcer could dub those words on the tape as the graphic appears. This "traditional" approach works well in formal topics, or when the client wants a serious treatment of the subject matter. But maybe your client recognizes that most of his sandwich shop workers are high school and college students. They might respond better to a humorous opening. You could produce a brief scenario involving what would happen if the sandwich was prepared incorrectly, with the roast beef sliding off the bread and the condiments dripping on the floor. The flip side of this comical introduction could show the correctly made sandwich being enjoyed by a customer. Showing the desired end product is a good way to begin an instructional program.

An even more serious approach than the "traditional" opening would be the exposure of the problem that resulted in this program being produced. A program could begin with magazine articles and statistics about food poisoning resulting from poorly prepared food. Whatever the approach, it is easy to see that the beginning of the instructional video program performs two important tasks: 1) It tells the viewer what task(s) will be learned and 2) it sets the tone for the program to follow.

The "middle" of an instructional video program contains most of the information that the producer wishes to communicate. The body of the video program contains all of the audio and video that are essential to learning the desired task. Narration and graphics are used to reinforce the content. As you complete this lesson, you will see how the body is shaped into effective video communication.

The end, or conclusion of an instructional video program, like the beginning, can take many forms. A review of the pertinent points of the procedure makes a great conclusion. Try to summarize the entire program in your concluding sentences. Show the finished product and the rewards for a job well done. A return to the introduction gives the viewer a sense of closure and completion. Remember, the conclusion makes a lasting impression on the viewer and sets the tone for the execution of the task. While "How to Kick a Soccer Ball" might end with people playing their favorite sport, "How to Jump-Start Your Car" should end on a more serious note.

To borrow an old adage from public speaking: Tell them what you're going to tell them, tell them, and then tell them what you told them!

# Planning an Instructional Video Program

Like any other video program, an instructional video program takes careful planning. Unlike other forms of presentation, the instructional video has a specific behavior to teach and reinforce. The instructional video planning session must strive for completeness as well as presentation.

The first step in most instructional videos involves diagnosing or identifying the problem. One fine student-produced instructional video is called "How to Add Oil to Your Car." You might think that this student production group's first instruction was "open the oil bottle" or "take off the oil cap." But this perceptive group went back to the beginning. They told the viewer how he or she would know that the car needed oil. The students videotaped someone routinely checking the oil level under the hood and even showed the illuminated "oil" light on the dashboard. (Actually, the "oil" light was a mock-up using red plastic and a penlight flashlight.)

Another important step to include in an instructional video program is the gathering of the appropriate materials. Along with showing an oil funnel and a towel to wipe up any spills, the student group also videotaped a student reading the car owner's manual to determine the correct type of oil for the car. Naturally, the task is not completed until all of the tools used are cleaned and prepared for the next use. Oily rags can start a fire, and the improper storage of unused oil can be messy and dangerous. The philosophy behind instructional video is that it is always the "maid's day off," so show the viewers how to complete the task. Don't leave them hanging!

Earlier, we mentioned the need to assess the level of the learner. When planning your instructional video, be aware of what the viewer does or does not already know about the topic. If in doubt, assume that your viewer knows little or nothing about your topic. It is better to have a few informed viewers bored during a minute of background information than to have most of your viewers confused by a program that assumes information not known or tasks not yet mastered. (Just why *do* cars need oil, anyway?) Remember, if in doubt, write it out!

Storyboarding is the next step. Lesson 4 fully explained the concept of storyboarding. As you can imagine, storyboarding is very important in the creation of instructional video programs. The omission of a single shot can make your video program incomplete, confusing, and ineffective. Besides making sure that every shot is completed, there are some general rules for storyboarding an instructional video program.

1. *Display your task from many different angles* (figure 1.45). Try to think of all of the camera angles you can possibly use for your project. Remember, each different camera angle might add new information to your program. A long shot is good for establishing the scene.

Fig. 1.45. Experimenting with a different camera angle.

Close-ups mixed with medium shots can give the viewer a sense of participation. Overhead shots can give the viewer an unobstructed view. Creativity is a big plus in instructional video. One student decided to make an instructional video program on "How to Bag Groceries." His objective was to show the viewer how to effectively use the space in the grocery bag while making sure not to crush the more fragile items. After videotaping several shots from various camera angles, he carefully cut the bottom out of the grocery bag. Then he put a piece of plexiglass between two tables and placed the bottomless bag on the plexiglass. Then, by positioning the camera on a tripod *underneath* the plexiglass, he created the unique "in-the-bag" camera angle that helped the viewer understand the exact positioning of each item in the grocery bag.

While the "different angles" approach leads to a more educational and watchable production, it does present one problem: the jump cut. A jump cut describes the situation in which a person or object "jumps" across the screen when a segment is edited. Let's go back to our example of adding oil to a car engine. Your first shot is your talent on camera sitting in the driver's seat of the car giving a 15-second intro to the program (figure 1.46). Your second shot shows your talent outside the car lifting the hood (figure 1.47). How did your talent magically jump from the inside to the outside of your car? This is a jump cut, and should be avoided. There are many solutions to this problem. Most are simple, but they need to be planned and storyboarded. You could end the first shot with the talent exiting the car and

**Fig. 1.46. Introducing the video program.**

**Fig. 1.47. A jump cut.**

walking off camera. Then the talent could walk into the second shot. Or, you could storyboard a graphic and edit it in between the first and second shots. This, in the mind of the viewer, would give the talent "time" to exit the car and walk around to the front. Carefully critique your storyboards and look for possible jump cuts. Even on television, viewers expect the world to make sense.

The concept of continuity also comes into play here. If a container of motor oil is opened in one shot, it cannot appear closed in the next shot. Even if videotaped on different days, your talent should be wearing the same clothing. And don't shift from day to evening scenes unless that time shift is important to your topic. Even though your shooting may take place in several locations over a period of a few days, your audience will feel more comfortable thinking that everything is happening as they are watching the program. Don't detract from your program by adding confusing jump cuts or continuity discrepancies. Consider assigning a detail-minded member of your group the task of keeping continuity on track and avoiding jump cuts in the raw footage.

2. *Make sure to show the appropriate detail that the viewer needs.* If the task involved requires manipulation of small items or the reading of print, you need to storyboard several macro-position shots to let your viewer get close to the action. Two students recently created an instructional video program on "How to Build Model Cars." They used many macro shots to let the viewer see the assembly of the small parts. Another popular project (because TV production class is often taught in the media center) is "How to Locate a Book in the Media Center." Whether using a traditional or electronic card cataloging system, the videographer needs to use the macro position to show the location of the information in the card catalog.

Showing the right details doesn't just mean using the macro lens of your camera or camcorder. Make sure to storyboard *all* of the concepts that you plan to mention in your script.

3. *Storyboard a "tips" section, if it applies to the topic.* Earlier we stated that an instructional video program should be more than just a series of tips. However, helpful hints are an important part of any program. Whether you offer this advice throughout the program, or at the end, make sure to let your personal experiences in the topic area work for the viewer. If you brainstorm, you can probably think of five or six helpful pieces of advice. Remember, the viewer may not have *any* experience with the task at hand.

4. *Storyboard the graphics.* Graphics are helpful tools for the instructional video producer. Plan for these graphics by determining the abilities of your character generator (number of lines, number of spaces per line, colors, etc.) and writing the graphics in a storyboard box just as you would storyboard any other shot. If you're following the project plan after this lesson, you will *not* be able to superimpose graphics over a camera shot. That's a more advanced skill. For now, plan to use letters on a solid background. Actually, this is a good technique for instructional videos. The switch from the camera shot to a solid background lets the viewer know that important information is about to be revealed. It also gives the viewer a sense of transition, allowing him or her to "shift gears" in the middle of the program.

5. Decide whether you will use live sound or do a total audio dub after the task is edited. There are advantages to each approach, and a combination of both can work well also. Live sound can work for an on-camera introduction and/or conclusion, and audio dub is best for the body of the program. The decision must be made in the storyboarding process, as it will affect your camera angle selection.

## Shooting the Instructional Video Program

After all this planning, actually shooting the raw footage may seem anticlimactic. Don't be fooled. Good camera work is the essence of an instructional video. And the best editing can't save terrible raw footage. The following tips should help.

1.  Use a tripod. A shaky camera can distract the viewer from the ever-important content. And with close-ups and macro shots, the camera exaggerates even slight motions.

2.  Avoid zooms and pans. These camera movements are distracting to the viewer trying to concentrate on learning a task. Establish your camera angle, then roll tape and perform the step of your task (figure 1.48). Move the camera, then roll tape again. Remember, you're not just performing the task in front of a camera. You're making a program that will teach a skill.

**Fig. 1.48. Establishing a camera angle.**
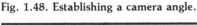

3.  Plan for several cycles of your task. If your task is "How to Make a Salad," you should bring duplicates of all of the ingredients so that your preparations can be videotaped from several angles. Once a tomato is sliced, it can't be put back together!

4.  Use your storyboards during the shoot. Don't rely on memory to supply the shots.

5.  Shoot to edit. If your class is following this text in order, this is the first project that you will be editing. Let the camera run a full *5 or 10 seconds* before you perform the task. Whether you're using the deck-to-deck editing system explained later, or a professional editing suite, you need that time to properly edit your shots. Also let the camera run a few seconds after the task is completed. Don't conserve videotape! Shoot the best, and edit the rest.

## Editing the Instructional Video Program

After all of your raw footage is shot and all of the graphics produced, you are ready to edit your program. If your school has a professional editing suite already in place, you probably won't have to worry about proper connections. But editing can be performed using two VCRs or even camcorders.

Videotape cannot be edited like film. If you have worked in film, from home Super 8mm to professional 35mm or 70mm, you know that film is edited by cutting, splicing, and taping or gluing the scenes together physically. In video, this is not possible. Cutting and pasting videotape has disastrous results. Film is actually a series of transparent pictures that is projected very quickly upon the screen. Videotape is magnetic, recording the signal onto the tape using electrical charges. One of the "tracks," or recording sections of a videotape is the control track (figure 1.49). Cutting the videotape will destroy the control track and ruin the project. Also, because videotape comes in direct contact with the VCR heads as it plays, a dab of film glue or splicing tape could ruin a VCR. To edit a videotape, you need two VCRs—one to play and another to record.

Fig. 1.49. Tracks on a videotape.

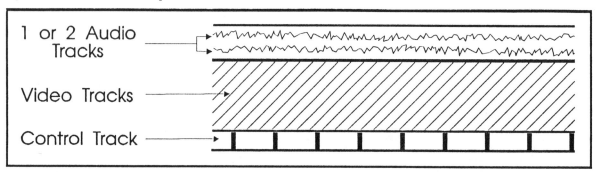

Because many schools don't have full editing suites, let's look at the proper connections to set up your own editing facility. Two simple rules apply.

Rule #1: Use four-head VCRs and camcorders when possible. This allows clear still-frame tape cuing and smoother edits.

Rule #2: Use only shielded cable in connecting these machines. This will give much cleaner tape-to-tape transfer.

To connect a simple deck-to-deck editing system, you need two video decks (or VCRs or camcorders), two televisions or monitors, and four or five lengths of shielded cable with connectors to fit your equipment. This connection is actually quite simple, and we'll break it into two parts: 1) connecting the VCRs to each other, and 2) connecting the VCRs to monitors or televisions.

*Connecting the VCRs to each other.* Set your VCRs on a table either side by side or, if ventilation is available, on top of one another. The left VCR, or top VCR will be your source (play) VCR and the right VCR or bottom VCR will be your record VCR (figure 1.50). This setup is standard in the industry and will avoid confusion if you have the opportunity to edit at another facility.

Next, locate the "video out" and "video in" jacks of your VCRs. Run a length of shielded cable from the "video out" jack of your source VCR to the "video in" jack of your record VCR. Your video connection is now complete.

Fig. 1.50. Deck-to-deck editing system connections.

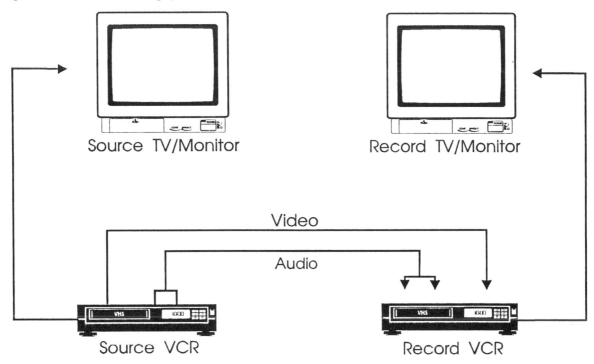

Now, locate the "audio in" and "audio out" jacks on the back of the VCRs. Run a length of shielded cable from the "audio out" jack of your source VCR to the "audio in" jack of your record VCR. If you are using stereo VCRs, there will be two sets of audio jacks, color-coded for left and right channels. Your audio connection is now complete.

*Connecting the VCRs to monitors or televisions.* Now, the only connection left to make is that between the monitors or televisions and the VCRs so that you can see the video being played/recorded on the VCRs (figure 1.51). First, determine if you have monitors or televisions. There are two major

Fig. 1.51. VCR-to-monitor connection.

differences: 1) Monitors have inputs for audio and video signals very similar to the jacks on the back of VCRs, while televisions have only the RF connector for composite audio/video signal; and 2) televisions have tuners (channel selectors) and monitors do not. Some people can argue for the advantages/disadvantages of monitors and televisions. Right now, it is really not that important. Monitors are connected to a "video out" of each VCR. This may pose a problem for your source VCR if you have only one "video out." If you are using televisions, connect them to the "RF out" of each VCR. (This will output video as well as audio—an advantage to using televisions.) How can you tell if your system is connected properly? A tape played in the source VCR should play through on both monitors/televisions.

*The deck-to-deck editing process.* The system that you have just created is called a deck-to-deck editing system, because you are editing from one VCR to another without the aid of an editing control unit. If you do have an editing control unit, the connection is the same, with the connection of the control unit to the VCRs. This lesson teaches the technique of deck-to-deck editing without an editing control unit.

Remember the concept of editing videotape: Videotape cannot be cut and spliced together like film. In order to combine and rearrange scenes, you must make a duplicate of the tape, copying the scenes in the correct order.

First, load the tape onto which you want to edit into the record VCR (right or bottom). This tape should be blank, or at least have a few minutes of blank tape left on it. Remember: You cannot edit a scene *before* another scene. This will destroy the control track.

It is nice to have a few seconds of black or neutral screen before your program begins. Blank videotape is not black and silent, but snow and "white noise." Our first edit then, will be this "black." Do you have a "black" tape? You should. A black tape is a videotape onto which a black screen has been recorded with no sound. To create a black tape, record a videotape in a camera or camcorder with the lens cap on, the iris closed, or the camera pointed at a piece of black material hanging on the wall. To eliminate the sound, attach an adapter, but no microphone, to the "mic" jack of your camcorder. If you have a character generator, you can record a black screen. A black tape is usually kept at the editing station for this purpose. Pull out the erase tab so that no one can record on the black tape.

Load the black tape into the source (left or top) VCR. Now each VCR has a videotape loaded. By using the record VCR controls, find the place that you want to begin creating your new program. Put the record VCR on "record" and "pause." Now, push "play" on the source VCR to begin playing the black tape. Push "pause" on the record VCR to start the recording tape rolling. Both televisions/monitors should display the black video. After you have recorded 15 or 20 seconds of the black tape, pause the record VCR, then stop the play VCR. Eject the black tape from the play VCR, while leaving the record VCR on record/pause. Now, find the first scene of your instructional video (use your storyboards!) and load that tape into the source VCR. When you find the proper starting point, put the source VCR on "play/pause." Your record VCR should still be on "record/pause." (*Note:* Most VCRs will hold a tape on pause for only a few minutes. Until you master the deck-to-deck editing technique, your record VCR may automatically stop while you are cuing your next scene. You *must* re-cue the record tape if it turns off automatically. Pushing record/play again is not enough. Even an inch of blank tape can ruin 10 seconds of edited project.) Now both VCRs are on their respective play or record and on pause. Un-pause both VCRs to get the tapes rolling. But which VCR is rolled first? The source or play VCR must be un-paused *slightly* before the record VCR. This will ensure the recording of rolling tape. If the record VCR rolls before the play VCR, you will be recording a second of still frame. This technique may be desirable, but at this point it is an error. After the segment that you wish to edit is complete, pause the record VCR, then the play VCR. Once again, this will ensure that you do not record a paused image. Now you have completed your first edit! Load/cue your next scene and get to work. When your program is complete, run more black, so that your viewer will not be exposed to the flash and loud noise of blank tape after the program is finished.

What happens if you allow more of your source video to be recorded than you intended? You need to re-cue your record tape so that the unintended segment will be recorded over on your next edit.

Let's review the procedure for a deck-to-deck edit:

1. Place the source tape in the play VCR and the tape onto which you will be recording into the record VCR.

2. Cue each tape.

3. Put the source tape on play/pause and the record tape on record/pause.

4. Un-pause the source VCR, and then un-pause the record VCR.

5. Allow the segment to be recorded.

6. Pause the record VCR, then pause or stop the source VCR.

7. Leave the record VCR on record/pause. Find your next scene on the source VCR.

8. Repeat the process for each subsequent scene.

Following are some deck-to-deck editing tips:

• Log each source tape that you use. Write down each shot and its approximate length.

• If possible, use a separate tape for graphics and each scene that you record. This will eliminate much of your rewinding and fast-forwarding. For example, if "How to Add Oil to Your Car" has scenes shot in the parking lot, scenes shot in the auto parts store, and graphics, it would be easier to use three separate tapes.

• Become adept at using your VCR's "search" functions. They will help you quickly locate shots.

• Be patient. It takes a few edits to master the technique. Before long you will be editing like a pro!

Here are some content suggestions:

• Beware of jump cuts. If a jump cut is inevitable, use a graphic to make the transition.

• Some VCRs have slow-motion and still-frame (clear, clean pause) capabilities. These can be used effectively, but are prone to abuse. Ask yourself, "Do I need to slow this down for viewers to understand?" If the answer is "yes," use your slow motion. Two students recently used slow motion quite effectively in a video entitled "How to Stepdance." Close-ups of dancing feet were slowed to show the viewer each subtle movement.

• Remember to intermingle shots of various angles and distances to maintain viewer interest. The first shot of each new scene is called an establishing shot, and makes the viewer aware of the location. In "How to Add Oil to Your Car," the students used an exterior shot of the auto parts store to begin the "shopping" section.

• Consider a "built-in pause" section in your instructional video if the tape is designed to be played while the viewer performs the task. For example, a viewer might watch "How to Knit" while holding yarn and knitting needles. One of the first techniques explained would be casting on—the process of weaving the yarn onto a knitting needle. After this process is shown and explained, you might want to add a 30-second shot of the completed cast-on while you narrate, "This is what your knitting needle should look like. If it doesn't look this way, rewind the tape and view this section again." After the completed cast-on is on the screen for about

30 seconds, continue the process of knitting with your next shot. A graphics screen can be substituted for the extended shot.

- Remember to make the video flow smoothly. Experiment with timing. A shot shown for too long bores the viewer, while the quick shot confuses.

## Audio-Dubbing Your Instructional Video Program

After you have edited your instructional video program, you need to complete the audio portion. The audio can either make or break an instructional video. The two parts of the audio discussed here are script and the audio-dub process.

*The script.* A good script can explain the task at hand and reinforce the video. A poor script can overwhelm and confuse. Follow this advice.

Guide the viewer through the program using the script. The narrator should convey a friendly and helpful tone. Write in second-person, active voice to draw the viewer into the project. For example, "Oil is now added to the driver's car" becomes "Now, slowly pour the oil into your car." Avoid "Here you see ..." phrasings. Make the viewer the active participant.

Use the script to explain any activities that are not clear within the video. Practice reading the script to achieve an appropriate balance. Too much script is overwhelming, and too little script leaves the viewer with a feeling of abandonment. Don't add useless or trivial information. Stay focused. Remember, the task may be entirely new to the viewer. Finally, write the script in the appropriate style. As discussed above, some topics require a formal treatment while others can take a more casual tone.

*The audio-dub process.* After the program is planned, shot, edited, and scripted, many students "see the light at the end of the tunnel" and subsequently do a sloppy job of audio-dubbing. But if you have properly shot and edited your video, your viewer will expect a professional audio track to match.

Practice reading your script aloud. Don't mumble your way through it. Like it or not, your audience will judge your professionalism based on your script delivery. And you can't truly practice script reading silently. Say the script aloud many times. Write your script on notecards. The microphone will pick up rustling papers. Numbering the notecards will help keep them in order. Choose an appropriate voice style. If the topic is serious, speak in a serious tone. Use a casual tone for lighter topics.

Music is important and should be chosen with the topic of the video in mind. A fast, rock-and-roll tune might work for "How to Skateboard" but would probably be out of place in "How to Arrange Flowers."

Instrumental music usually works best, but vocals are not out of the question. Check soundtracks and jazz collections for good instrumentals, and avoid songs with strong vocals that will usually overwhelm the narrator. Also beware of lyrics that have absolutely nothing to do with the topic. The Beach Boys' "Sail on Sailor" would be great for a videotape titled "How to Prepare for a Day of Sailing" but would be out of place in "How to Scramble Eggs." Don't forget to pay careful attention to the mixing levels. While the song may be really great, it is *never* more important than the script.

Did you use "live" on-camera sound during your instructional video? *Do not* audio-dub over that sound. It will be erased. *Before you begin* your audio dub, play your tape through and note the counter number when your live sound begins. Stop the audio-dubbing VCR when that number approaches. Then, resume your audio dub at the next section. Audio-dubbing erases the existing audio track. And once it's gone, it's gone!

Instructional video production is fun and rewarding. As each member of your class creates a different project, you will learn new skills and probably be impressed at just how much your friends know! Instructional video production is also a useful job skill for those interested in video as a career.

# Review Questions: Lesson 6

1. How do modern instructional video programs differ from classroom programs created in the early days of television?

2. What type of topics work best in instructional video programs?

3. What type of topics do not work very well in instructional video programs?

4. What does it mean to say that an instructional video program should be "narrow in scope"?

5. What two things are done by the introduction of an instructional video program?

6. What is the first step in planning an instructional video program?

(Review questions continue on page I-1-90.)

7. If you don't know the learning level of your viewer, what assumption should you make?

8. How can jump cuts be avoided?

9. What is the best way to avoid continuity problems?

10. Why can't videotape be edited with the cut-and-paste method?

11. In deck-to-deck editing systems _____ VCRs and _____ cable should be used.

12. When arranging VCRs in the deck-to-deck configuration, which VCR should be on the left or on the top?

    Which one should be on the right or bottom?

13. When should a "built-in pause" be used in instructional video programs?

# *Activities: Lesson 6*

1.  Visit your local video rental store or public library. Make a list of 10 instructional videotapes available.

2.  Using the *TV Guide* or another TV listing, make a list of the instructional video programs available on television.

3.  Ask your school media specialist what topics are covered by the school's collection of instructional videotapes.

4.  Using a magazine about video programs, find the most popular instructional video program. How much does it cost?

5.  Visit a local business and ask if they use videotape to train their employees. (Tip: fast-food restaurants use video to train employees.) Ask to see one of these programs.

6.  Ask one of your teachers about tasks that they would like to have made into instructional video programs.

7.  Watch an instructional videotape program. Does the program use the same techniques discussed in this lesson?

8.  After you have become a skilled editor, create a short program packed full of jump cuts and continuity problems. Show it to your friends and ask them to make a list of all the problems they see.

9.  Watch the movie *Plan 9 from Outer Space,* commonly known as the worst movie of all time because of its continuity problems. Make a list of the production problems. (And be prepared to make a long list!)

## Student Project Plan: Instructional Video Program

### DESCRIPTION OF COMPLETED PROJECT

The completed project will be a 3- to 5-minute videotape program instructing the audience on a certain task. The project must include at least five different camera angles, music, titles, end credits, and internal graphics.

### METHOD

1.  Students will choose a task and list the steps needed to accomplish the task.
2.  Students will storyboard the project.
3.  Students will generate graphics and record them. At least three pages of graphics must be used: a title, an end credit ("Produced by ... "), and at least one page of graphics to be used within the program to help the viewer learn the task.
4.  Students will shoot the raw footage.
5.  Students will edit the raw footage, making the program.
6.  Students will audio-dub the program by adding narration and music where needed.

### EQUIPMENT

audio mixer

camera and deck or camcorder

character generator

microphone

music sources

tripod

two TVs/monitors

two VCRs

### EVALUATION

The project will be worth 200 points. Each team member will receive the same score.

| | |
|---|---|
| instructional value | (50) |
| graphics | (25) |
| audio | (25) |
| editing | (25) |
| camera work | (25) |
| script | (25) |
| storyboards | (25) |

## *Evaluation Sheet: Instructional Video Program*

STUDENTS _____

Period _____

Total Points _____ %

Letter grade  A    B    C    D    Re-do

**Instructional value** (50 points)

| | | |
|---|---|---|
| Appropriate task | (10) | _____ |
| Step-by-step process | (10) | _____ |
| Appropriate rate | (10) | _____ |
| Did we learn? | (20) | _____ |

                                                      Total   (50)   _____

**Graphics** (25 points)

| | | |
|---|---|---|
| Title screen | (5) | _____ |
| Internal graphics | (10) | _____ |
| Credits | (5) | _____ |
| Color contrast | (5) | _____ |

                                                      Total   (25)   _____

**Audio** (25 points)

| | | |
|---|---|---|
| Mixing levels | (10) | _____ |
| Narration performance | (5) | _____ |
| Music selection | (5) | _____ |
| Overall polish | (5) | _____ |

                                                      Total   (25)   _____

(Evaluation Sheet continues on page I-1-94.)

**Editing** (25 points)

|              |      |            |
|--------------|------|------------|
| Technical quality | (10) | _____ |
| Program length | (10) | _____ |
| Pace | (5) | _____ |

                              Total   (25)   _____

**Camera work** (25 points)

|              |      |            |
|--------------|------|------------|
| Shot selection | (10) | _____ |
| Five angles | (5) | _____ |
| Focus | (5) | _____ |
| Appropriate detail | (5) | _____ |

                              Total   (25)   _____

**Script** (25 points)

|              |      |            |
|--------------|------|------------|
| Appropriate amount | (10) | _____ |
| Good explanation | (10) | _____ |
| Appropriate style | (5) | _____ |

                              Total   (25)   _____

**Storyboards** (25 points)

|              |      |            |
|--------------|------|------------|
| Completion | (15) | _____ |
| Visual | (5) | _____ |
| Audio | (5) | _____ |

                              Total   (25)   _____

# Lesson 7 Multicamera Small Studio Production

## Objectives

After successfully completing this lesson, you will be able to:

- *connect the equipment needed for a talk show.*
- *understand and execute basic camera movements using a tripod.*
- *select an appropriate guest for a talk show.*
- *formulate good questions for a talk show.*
- *write a good introduction and conclusion for a talk show.*
- *design a simple talk show set.*
- *successfully complete a talk show assignment.*

## Vocabulary

**Cut.** A video transition in which one video source instantly and completely replaces another video source.

**Dissolve.** A video transition in which one video source fades out as another video source fades in.

**Dolly.** A camera movement in which the camera is rolled on a tripod dolly or studio pedestal toward the subject ("dolly in") or away from the subject ("dolly out").

**Electronic field production (EFP).** Complex video production outside the television production studio. EFP is more elaborate and involves more equipment than ENG.

**Fade.** A video transition in which one video source is gradually replaced on the screen by a background color. A fade is a dissolve to a background color.

**Follow-up.** A question in an interview based on the answer to a previously answered question.

**Pan.** A side-to-side camera movement as the camera base remains stationary.

**Tilt.** A vertical camera movement as the camera base remains stationary.

**Tripod dolly.** A tripod mounted on a dolly base ("spreader").

**Truck.** A lateral movement of the camera achieved by moving the tripod dolly or studio pedestal to the left ("truck left") or to the right ("truck right").

**Wipe.** A video transition in which one video source is replaced by another video source with a definite line of transition.

Many of the longest-running and most successful programs on television are talk shows. Whether the topic is political, social, or purely entertaining, talk shows continue to gain popularity in many time slots throughout the nation. We know our favorite talk show hosts by their first names—Phil, Oprah, Arsenio, Jay, Geraldo, Sally Jesse.

Talk shows are usually relatively inexpensive to produce because they don't require lengthy scripts or exotic settings. Although talk shows may not require a great deal of technical preproduction, they do provide an opportunity for spontaneous, "as-it-happens" television production work. At the outset of the program, no one involved knows exactly what will happen. Prepared and professional television production personnel can make the talk show happen, capturing that controversial comment or getting a reaction shot that really tells the story.

While most professional talk shows are produced in elaborate television studios, schools can produce talk shows in their studios or by configuring ENG equipment. While many schools have television production studios, many do not. The next few paragraphs describe assembling your equipment into a working, talk show studio.

## Equipment Connections

The equipment connection for a talk show is very similar to the connection for the "News Brief" student project plan described in lesson 5. The only addition is a second (and possibly third) camera and a microphone for each participant. Figure 1.52 illustrates such a connection, with the necessary additions, to help in this process. Remember, alternate connections can be made, depending on the availability of equipment. If you aren't ready to turn back to lesson 5 right now, the process is as follows. For video, connect both camera outputs to the inputs of the switcher. The video output of the switcher is daisy-chained through the character generator and the signal is sent to the record VCR. For audio, all audio inputs (mics and music) are connected to the audio mixer. That audio signal is sent to the record VCR. Audio and video monitors are used where appropriate.

Fig. 1.52. Talk show equipment connections.

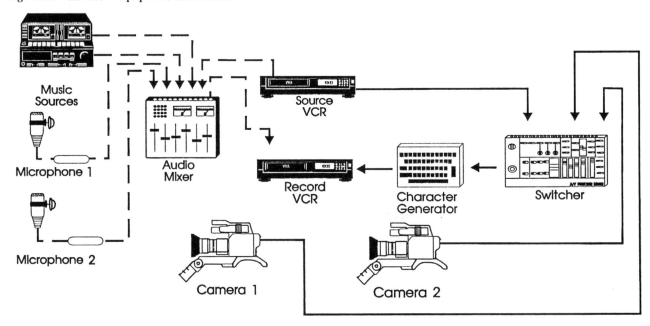

Obviously, if you have a television production studio in your school, you will use this for your talk show. However, the configured ENG system can be great for producing remote talk shows. This type of video work—assembling studio or ENG components for production in the field, is called EFP, or electronic field production. EFP differs from ENG in the complexity of the equipment taken into the field. A reporter conducting a brief interview, recorded by a single camera operator, is ENG. A video production team using two cameras, a switcher, a character generator, and an audio mixer to record an academic awards assembly is EFP.

## Tripods

Tripods help the videographer achieve a steady shot during program production. The tripod provides a firm base and tireless service not otherwise possible. Even the strongest, most experienced videographers cannot be expected to hold a steady shot for more than a minute or two.

Tripods also facilitate smooth camera movement. The four camera movements most often associated with tripods are pans, tilts, dollies, and trucks. *Panning* a camera means moving the camera from side to side on the tripod. During a pan, the tripod remains stationary. The camera pans atop the tripod. Pans are useful when following the action, showing the expanse of a shot, or making minor adjustments in the picture composition. But pans should not be used to "look" for a good shot. All pans used in a video program should have a purpose.

A *tilt* is similar to a pan, except that in a tilt, the camera motion is vertical, not horizontal, atop the tripod. Like pans, tilts should be used to emphasize the height of the subject, or to make a minor adjustment in the composition.

Many tripods can be fitted with wheels or casters to allow the tripod to roll smoothly across the floor. This wheel or caster assembly is called a dolly, and the tripod becomes a tripod dolly when a dolly is attached. Dollies are also known as "spreaders" because many have the ability to adjust, or "spread," to meet the tripod's base. Moving the tripod dolly toward the talent or away from the talent is called *dollying*. A lateral (side-to-side) motion of the tripod dolly is called a *truck*. Videographers can be instructed to "dolly forward," "dolly back," "truck left," or "truck right."

Many tripods and tripod dollies used in television production have a special means for attaching the camera to the tripod. The quick-release assembly is quite common. Screwing the camera into a tripod can be a time-consuming, knuckle-bruising experience. These quick-release methods save time and effort. The tripod includes a special plate or post assembly that screws into the bottom of the camera (figure 1.53). That plate or post can be quickly and conveniently attached to the tripod (figure 1.54). Most video production tripods now incorporate such a device.

If possible, select a tripod that doesn't have too many loose parts. In school television production, students often work against the 50-minute class period. Small parts that are easily detached from the tripod can quickly become lost. If you have the opportunity, select a tripod that doesn't easily disassemble itself!

## Preproduction Activities

As mentioned earlier, talk shows are often unpredictable and spontaneous. While some things are out of the production team's control, careful attention to preproduction details can help the team be ready for those unexpected moments.

Unless your talk show topic requires a specific guest, carefully select the person who will appear on your show. Choose someone who is interested in the topic, usually answers questions in complete sentences, and uses proper grammar and words that your audience can understand. Perhaps most important, choose someone who really wants to help with the program. Many students in the past have begged popular teachers and students to appear on a talk show, only to have the guest cancel at the last minute or provide lackluster conversation.

(Text continues on page I-1-99.)

Fig. 1.53. Plate assembly for tripod.

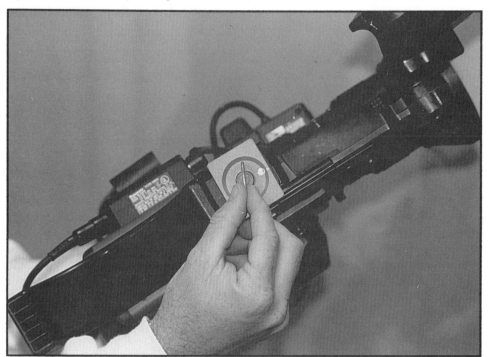

Fig. 1.54. Attaching plate assembly to tripod.

Application of the above criteria means that production teams will usually, but not always, choose adults as talk-show guests. (Some student guests can handle a 15-minute conversation *and* the distraction of the television crew and equipment.) Don't forget about community members who can help with this project. Doctors, police officers, paramedics, crisis counselors, and airline pilots are among the most memorable guests. One group even coordinated a visit by the local Guardian Angels.

It is wise to remember that most people have an interesting story to tell. One group surprised many classmates by introducing one of the school cafeteria workers as a guest. Instead of a conversation about school food preparation, the audience was treated to a conversation about the worker's religious missionary experience in Africa. Another group interviewed a school custodial worker about his experiences in the Pacific during World War II. A good host looks beneath the surface to find the best topic for discussion.

Obviously, it is important to determine the main topic of discussion for your interview and stay with that topic until it has been covered exhaustively. One group interviewed the head football coach, who is also a driver education instructor at the school. The first question was "What can we expect from the football team this year?" The second question was "What is the most important thing a student can learn in driver's ed?" You can probably imagine the mental whiplash experienced by both the guest and the audience. Within the course of a 15-minute talk show, the program can reasonably cover two, or maybe even three, topic areas. But those topics should not be intermingled within the program.

Once the host determines the topic area, he or she should formulate a list of questions to ask during the program. Generally, there are two types of questions: open-ended questions and closed-ended questions. Closed-ended questions can be answered with one or two words. "What is your favorite class in school?" is a closed-ended question. Your guest could answer in one word. Another closed-ended question is "Do you like your job?" By using only closed-ended questions, the interviewer could easily ask question #100 5 minutes into the program! In order to remedy this, some talk show hosts tack on "Why?" to the closed-ended question. Although this might extend the answer, asking "Why?" after each response will probably put the guest on the defensive and result in a cross-examination style of interview.

The solution to the closed-ended question is not to ask "Why?" but to use the open-ended question instead. The open-ended question inherently requires explanation and elaboration. "How can a person become an airline pilot?" is an example of an open-ended question. Instead of asking "Do you like your job?" ask "When did you receive the most satisfaction from your job?"

Usually, the open-ended question will lead to a follow-up question. A follow-up question is a question that is based on the answer to a previous question. For example, the question "How can a person become an airline pilot?" can lead to the follow-up question "How important was your military service to obtaining your pilot's license?" An alert talk show host will listen to the answers and ask questions that the audience would want to ask if they could. In other words, they *talk* with the guest. One talk show host asked a doctor what influenced her to enter the medical profession. The guest replied that she was inspired by the poor medical conditions in her homeland. Without missing a beat, the talk show host turned a routine interview on careers in medicine into a 20-minute dialogue on medical conditions in third-world countries.

Great questions and inquisitive follow-ups will mean nothing if the viewer is not paying attention to the program. A carefully crafted introduction will capture the audience's attention and draw them into the program. An all-too-common opening sounds like this: "Hi, we're here today with Ms. Nancy Lugo, who is a counselor at the crisis center." On the surface, that sounds OK. But it really does nothing to bring the viewer into the program; the viewer should feel that he or she has a personal stake in the program. Let's try another introduction: "Have you ever felt depressed? Did you ever think that there was no one to turn to? Well, there's always someone to listen. Someone who cares is just a phone call away. Nancy Lugo is one of those people who will listen to you, and she's our guest today."

A successful talk show needs a strong conclusion that will summarize and further personalize the interview. "Well, that's all the time we have today ..." is commonly used, and doesn't end the show on a positive note. The conclusion should be mentally prepared by the host throughout the program. The host can even jot down a word or two on a small notepad while the camera is on a close-up of the guest. Our interview with the crisis counselor might conclude: "If you ever need to talk to someone, you can call Nancy Lugo and her friends at The Crisis Hotline at 555-1234. Remember, no problem is too large or too small. Thank you very much for joining us today, Ms. Lugo. For Campus Outlook, I'm Adam Whiteside." A good interview deserves a good conclusion!

All interviews need a place to happen. A good talk show set can add tremendously to your program, and it really isn't as hard to create as it sounds (figure 1.55). The first thing to remember in set creation is that you really only need to worry about what the camera sees. A simple, two-person talk show set is really quite small—about 10 feet wide, 6 or 7 feet high, and 5 or 6 feet deep. As long as the camera remains within these boundaries, your set design need not extend beyond this minimal area.

Fig. 1.55. Talk show set.

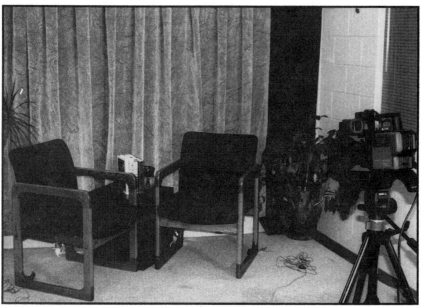

Office or reception-area chairs work well for a talk show. Remember to place the chairs close together to avoid too much empty space on the set. A background can be fashioned from a curtain, a set of miniblinds, or even bulletin board paper. Try to avoid the extremes of black and white when selecting your background.

Your set can be "dressed" to give it the "living room" approach. Potted plants give the set color and warmth. Hardbound books on a small end table and natural artifacts, such as rocks, seashells, and potted plants, can also dress the set. A bookcase filled with books and knickknacks works well. Use your imagination to create a simple, yet effective set.

Lighting the set can be achieved in many different ways. For many newer video cameras, the natural classroom lighting, combined with light coming through doors and windows, can create enough illumination. Simple clip lights, available at most hardware stores for a few dollars, can illuminate the dark parts of the set and provide backlight. Small professional light kits, usually containing two or three lights on stands, are available for a few hundred dollars. Such purchases represent a wise investment for schools producing talk shows on a regular basis. Remember to white-balance your cameras *after* your artificial lights have been turned on. Different types of light can drastically change the color response of your cameras.

Some other important preproduction notes: Carefully consider the host's wardrobe for the show. Scruffy jeans or shorts generally look sloppy on camera, especially in light of the complexity of this assignment. Men should consider wearing a tie, and ladies a dress or skirt/blouse ensemble. Remember to dress on the level of your guest; an off-campus guest may be wearing a business suit. Also, encourage your guest to wear his or her uniform if it will add to the atmosphere of your program.

Paramedics, police officers, and firefighters are just a few of the uniformed professionals who will make your viewers sit up and watch.

Storyboard the basic shots that you want in your interview program. This simple task will probably take only a few minutes, but will dispel any confusion about the "look" of your show. Will your talk show feature medium shots and bust shots, or two-shots and close-ups? Carefully consider the types of shots you want to use in your program.

**Fig. 1.56. Crossing pattern.**

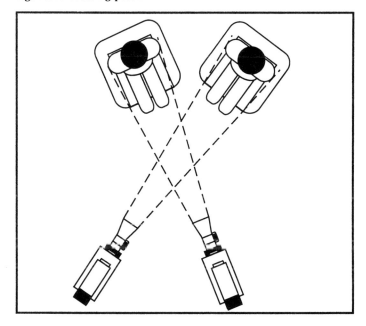

Plan to shoot the program with two cameras in a "crossing pattern," as shown in Figure 1.56. In other words, the camera on the left should get the close-up of the person on the right, and the camera on the right should get the close-up of the person on the left. This approach will achieve the 45-degree profile desired for a talk show. A left camera/left guest approach gives a full profile, and is often disorienting to the viewer.

Plan which channels on your audio mixer you will be using for your talk show. For a simple program, you will need two "mic" channels and one music source channel. Determine the audio mixing levels *before* the show begins.

Probably the most important aspect of preproduction is working as a team. Unfortunately, this aspect is almost indefinable. But there are some tips to follow. Make sure to listen to all members of the group when making decisions, and be willing to compromise with all members of your group. Everyone in your group will have something to offer. Remember: In a good working group, the final product is more than the sum of the parts. Make sure that you are contributing to further the goal of the group—to make a great talk show program.

## Production Activities

Many schools have access to a character generator. Generated titles can make your program appear more professional. Plan to use a title for your talk show. Use the last line of your character generator page to create "name tags" for the talk show host and guest(s). Superimpose these graphics over the first few close-ups of your host and guest(s). Display the graphics long enough for the viewer to read them—very slowly. Use the graphics again near the middle and end of the program. Create a separate page for credits, and display that page after the talk show is complete.

Once your guest and host are seated on the set, establish the shots storyboarded in your planning sessions. Make sure to allow the correct amount of noseroom in your close-ups. Practice directing the camera operators and switcher. Common director commands are "Ready to cut to camera 1. Go 1." "Dissolve to camera 2. Go 2." The team should become accustomed to giving and taking directions without bruising every ego.

Some sort of communication system is needed between the director, the switcher, and the videographers. The audio technician and the graphics generator also need to be in communication with the director. The two most common types of communication systems are wired and wireless intercom systems. Wireless intercom systems use radio frequencies that broadcast between the units (figure 1.57).

Fig. 1.57. Wireless intercom system.

The range and quality vary by manufacturer. When using wireless intercom systems, check the frequency of the system against the frequency of a wireless microphone system you may be using. The wireless microphone system receiving station will receive any signals broadcast on that frequency, including the signals generated by the wireless intercom. Wireless intercom systems can be used when using intercom cable is impractical (across a gymnasium floor) or impossible (communicating across a lake or river). Wired intercom systems are usually more expensive and durable. Most professional cameras and switchers have built-in wired intercom systems already in place.

During production the switcher can perform transitions between shots. The most basic transition, a *cut*, is simply replacing the first shot with the second shot. A cut usually involves pushing the desired button on the same *bus* or row of buttons. A *dissolve* slowly replaces the first shot with the second. As the first shot fades out, the second shot fades in. A third type of transition is a *wipe*. A wipe replaces the second shot with the first shot with a definite line. This wipe could go from top to bottom, side to side, corner to corner, etc. Many modern production switchers have 50 or more different wipe patterns. The final type of transition, used at the beginning and end of the program, is a *fade*. A fade is a dissolve that changes from the first shot to a background color. That color is often black. But many switchers allow fading to an infinite number of background colors.

You may choose the option of rolling videotape from a separate VCR into your talk show. For example, during an interview with the football coach, the talk show production crew may want to include videotape of a scoring drive and have the coach describe what's happening on the field. The source VCR should be connected to the switcher just as the cameras are connected. Then at the appropriate time, the tape in the source VCR can be played as the switcher selects the appropriate source. Rolling footage can make the talk show more entertaining and informative.

Before the show begins, plan a signal to let the host know how much time is left in the program. On shows requiring exact times, a darkroom timer can be used. If the program has no maximum time limit, a signal can be devised to inform the host when the minimum time for the program has been reached. Make sure that the guest knows the signal, too. Waving a red handkerchief may seem like a good way to tell the host when she has reached the 15-minute mark. But it may confuse, confound, or even panic the unsuspecting guest. What would you think if you were the guest on a talk show and a camera operator began waving a bandanna?

More sophisticated shows may want to add the audience participation aspect. This should be attempted only after the team becomes quite experienced at talk show production. Consider the studio audience as extra guests on your show. You need to be concerned with lighting, camera angles, and the appearance of your studio audience members. If you plan to have an audience participation portion of the talk show, you need to plan camera angles and microphone access. While this approach can have impressive results, proper execution requires meticulous planning, experience, and professionalism.

Producing a talk show is a fun, entertaining way to display your television production expertise (figure 1.58). With correct equipment connection, preproduction teamwork, careful planning, and thoughtful production, the talk show can be a valuable experience in television production class.

Fig. 1.58. A television talk show.

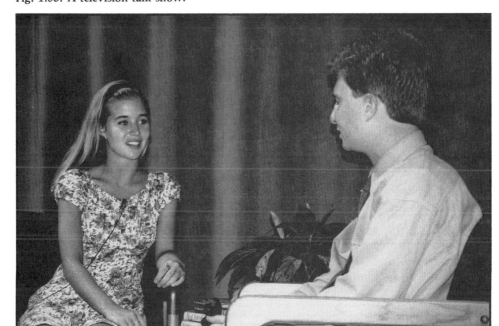

---

# Review Questions: Lesson 7

1.   What is EFP?


2.   What is the difference between ENG and EFP? Give an example of each.


3.   What are the four basic tripod dolly movements?


4.   List the criteria that should be applied in the guest selection process.


5.   What are the three types of questions used in interviews?


6.   Convert the following questions into open-ended questions.

   "Do you like your job?"


   "How many years have you lived here?"


   "How many years did you study to become a lawyer?"


   "Do you think people should vote in every election?"


7.   What is a follow-up question?

8.   What items can be used to decorate a set?

9.   What wardrobe guidelines should be used by talk show hosts?

10.   What does it mean to shoot in a "crossing pattern"?

11.   List the three ways graphics are used in a talk show.

12.   What are the two types of intercom systems used in talk shows?

13.   What is the difference between a dissolve and a fade?

14.   What new considerations are presented when the talk show includes audience participation?

## *Activities: Lesson 7*

1.  Write introductions for the following topics:

    school board member—requirements for graduation

    student body president—prom plans

    firefighter—career inquiry

2.  Write conclusions for the following topics:

    race car driver—most exciting moments

    school principal—scheduling classes for next year

    foreign exchange student—adjusting to life in the United States

3.  Watch your favorite talk show and complete the following activities:

    Storyboard four different camera angles used in the program.

    Analyze the introduction and conclusion used by the host.

    List three questions used by the talk show host.

    List follow-up questions used by the host.

4.  Survey the students and faculty at your school. Ask them to name their favorite talk show. Report the findings to the class.

5.  Find out which talk show is the highest-rated talk show in your area and in the nation.

6.  Find out which talk shows have won Emmy awards in recent years.

7.  Many talk shows, especially the ones that air in the mornings and afternoons, are syndicated. Find out what this means.

8.  Call a local television station and ask how much it spends on syndicated talk shows. Also ask how much it costs to buy a 30-second commercial during that talk show.

## Student Project Plan: Talk Show

### DESCRIPTION OF COMPLETED PROJECT

The completed project will be a 10- to 15-minute talk show. The program will be totally self-contained. The show will include opening music and graphics, two people on camera (the interviewer and guest) conducting an interview session, internal graphics featuring the names of the host and the guest, end credits, and music. The program will use two cameras and a switcher. No postproduction will be used.

### METHOD

1. Each student will select a job that best suits his or her educational goal: videographer, graphics, audio technician, switcher, host, production coordinator.

2. Students will be assigned to teams based on that interest.

3. Students will then plan the video project. Emphasis will be placed on selecting a guest who will give the program a professional demeanor.

4. Each group will have at least one class session to practice production skills as a team.

5. Each team will have one class session to videotape the program.

### EQUIPMENT

audio mixer

character generator

lavaliere microphones

monitors

music sources

switcher

tripods

two cameras

VCR

### EVALUATION

Each student in the group will receive an individual grade and a group grade. Each grade is 100 points, for a total of 200 points.

## *Evaluation Sheet: Talk Show*

SHOW TITLE _____

PRODUCTION DATE _____

| | Individual Grade | + | Group Grade | = | Total Grade |
|---|---|---|---|---|---|
| Host | _____ | | _____ | | _____ |
| Comments: | | | | | |
| Production Coordinator | _____ | | _____ | | _____ |
| Comments: | | | | | |
| Switcher | _____ | | _____ | | _____ |
| Comments: | | | | | |
| Audio | _____ | | _____ | | _____ |
| Comments: | | | | | |
| Graphics | _____ | | _____ | | _____ |
| Comments: | | | | | |
| Camera 1 | _____ | | _____ | | _____ |
| Comments: | | | | | |
| Camera 2 | _____ | | _____ | | _____ |
| Comments: | | | | | |

Instructor's Comments:

# 2 CURRICULUM INTEGRATION
## Videotaping School Events and Activities

### Objectives

After successfully completing this unit, you will be able to:

- *identify the equipment needed to videotape various types of school events and activities.*

- *successfully videotape a school event or activity.*

Television production students are often asked to assist teachers and other students in videotaping and producing videotapes for various school events and activities. These requests range from simply videotaping a classroom guest speaker or student classroom presentation to a multicamera event in the school auditorium. School plays, fashion shows, talent shows, athletic contests, and school award presentations are routinely videotaped and later shown to classes and school organizations. Television students properly trained in videotaping these events can be a valuable resource to the entire school, as well as the television production program.

Learning to professionally videotape these events and functions, along with the necessary skills and concepts needed to correctly hook up the equipment, can lead to career opportunities in the community. Hotels, motels, and convention sites provide these resources for guests and community groups and are willing to hire personnel trained in the audiovisual support services. Local production companies are also eager to hire well-trained and experienced videographers.

This chapter will provide you with the information and concepts required for successfully videotaping many school events and activities. Although the equipment models and facilities vary from school to school, the techniques remain the same.

## Classroom Applications

### Guest Speakers

A visit by a guest speaker, a common and enriching experience, allows teachers to utilize the talents and knowledge of citizens in the community to provide students with up-to-date information in their field of study. Videotaping your guest speaker has several advantages:

1.  It allows flexible scheduling for your speaker. Guests can choose the time that is best suited to their needs, rather than having to meet the teacher's request for a certain period or time.

2.  Speakers can be scheduled for small classroom situations rather than large auditorium settings.

3.  It allows you the opportunity to "revisit" a speaker with your class for discussion and comments. Students who were absent can also take the tape home to view when they return.

4.  Teachers can share their tapes and take advantage of each other's contacts in the community.

Generally, most guest speakers can be videotaped with a single-camera system. The equipment should include:

- video camera/deck system, or camcorder
- microphone and mic extension cable
- AC power adapter
- extension cord/gaffer's tape
- tripod
- headphones
- videotape

Most problems can be easily eliminated by following some simple guidelines.

- *Always use a tripod.* A steady camera is a must, and no one can hold a camera still during the length of time a speaker is presenting information to the class. Set your camera/tripod a comfortable distance from the speaker; close enough for a good shot but not so close that you will distract him or her during the presentation. Be aware of backlight and glare from classroom windows and lights. If there is to be interaction between guests and students, be sure you can pan to capture all areas of the class. Check with the speaker before the presentation to find out if there are visual aids that should be included in the videotaping.

- *Make sure you have an uninterrupted power source.* Batteries will often "die" at the most inopportune times. Use an alternating current (AC) power adapter for your power source. Use gaffer's tape or masking tape to tape down your extension cord in areas where people will be walking to prevent accidents and loss of power during taping.

- *Ensure that you have good sound.* Always use an external microphone. Don't rely on the internal camera microphone. A lavaliere mic can be attached to the speaker's clothes, or you may decide to use a shotgun microphone to capture a question-and-answer period with the class. Dynamic microphones placed on a floor or desk stand can also be used. Use headphones to monitor your sound as you are recording. (See part I, lesson 2, for a full explanation of microphones.)

- *Don't forget to label your videotape.* Include the speaker's name and title, topic, and teacher's name and date. When the videotaping is completed, you can add the length of the presentation.

Experiment and practice videotaping "speakers" in your television classroom. Review the tape with your teacher and classmates, identify areas that need improvement, and note outstanding sections. After a few sessions of taping, you will be developing your skills as professionals as well as building a valuable resource for your school.

## Lab/Science Experiments

A picture is worth a thousand words, and in 30 pictures per second (frames) a video can describe quite a bit in a short amount of time. A science experiment or lab can be difficult to describe, but easily shown on tape. Even procedures used in the lab (safety, setups, cleanups, emergency procedures, etc.) can be videotaped and shown periodically throughout the year. With the use of some simple editing, audio-dubbing, and additional graphics, these labs can be "saved" and used as needed.

Depending upon the type of situation you are videotaping (teacher demonstration, group work, experiments), some equipment considerations should include:

- camera setup
- microphones and mic cables
- tripod
- power source
- extension cords
- lights (if needed)
- videotape

The placement of cameras and possible use of a switcher depend upon the program you are taping. A teacher demonstration, for example, would be best videotaped using two cameras and a switcher. One camera would be set for a medium shot and another for close-ups of the activity being demonstrated. A lavaliere mic on the teacher would be sufficient for recording sound.

If a lab or experiment by a group of students is being taped by a single camera, the camera operator will need to move around and record from several angles. Some shots need to be close-ups, even macro shots, and others can be filmed at a medium distance from the students. For sound recording, a shotgun mic can capture all of the group's discussion, or a Pressure Zone Microphone© (PZM) placed on the table can be used. In this situation, there would be a need for editing to make a good copy for later use in the classroom.

In some cases, the use of simple lighting would assist in videotaping experiments and procedures. For close-ups and macro shots, the areas need to be well lit for videotaping. Classroom lighting is often not enough to adequately videotape these types of experiments.

Work closely with the science department at your school to identify what types of activities are scheduled that would be best to videotape and use for classroom instruction. Coordinate your activities to provide a situation that benefits both the science department and the television production program. You'll be able to develop your skills as a videographer and provide a teaching resource for your school.

# Athletic Events

Taping athletic events is rewarding to the videographer, the athlete, the coach, and the school. Careers in sports videography abound, and quite a few colleges will give full scholarships to "team managers," who are solely responsible for videotaping games and practices. In viewing the videotapes, the athlete can benefit by analyzing his or her performance, and the coaching staff can see how well their game strategy worked. Many athletic coaches review every game for strategy and to record game statistics. Sports highlights can be edited and audio-dubbed for viewing at the annual sports banquet. Television students gain valuable experience taping the games, and it makes great public relations material for the school. These highlights can be shown at awards banquets and booster club meetings and can be included in video yearbooks.

Sports activities that lend themselves best to videotaping include gymnastics, football, basketball, wrestling, diving, track, and cheerleading. These can easily be taped on a single-camera system. Baseball, volleyball, and softball are more difficult to tape with one camera due to the nature of the action of the game. Highlight tape is easily shot, but continuous play is more difficult.

One of the best ways to learn sports videotaping is to preview some games already taped and note specifics, like camera position, camera start/stop time, and game versus highlight taping. The following list of suggestions can assist you in videotaping athletic events at your school.

1. *Camera start/stop time.* Most camcorders/VCRs will "roll back" slightly each time the camera "record" button is pushed to stop recording. If the camera operator pushes the trigger at the end of each play, as the VCR rolls back, the last few seconds of each play will be erased. To avoid this, allow 3 to 5 seconds after the completion of a play, or event, before depressing the "record/pause" button. To avoid color bars from appearing in your sports highlights, start recording action 5-9 seconds before the start of each play.

2. *Camera positioning.* This will vary with each sport, but allow yourself to experiment and find the best angle to record the action, both on the field and in the stands. Some of your best footage will come from the reaction of fans, coaches, and players on the sidelines! Camera positioning varies with the purpose of the taping. Coaches will prefer wider-angle shots to view the position of all players on the field, whereas highlight taping looks best from close-ups and tighter shots that depict the intensity of the game.

3. *Scoreboard/Clock.* Most coaches prefer that the scoreboard be taped following time-outs and at the end of each period of play. In football, it is generally suggested that the videographer tape the scoreboard after each score. Gymnasts and wrestlers like to have their points taped after each event. Basketball, because of the nature of the game, has a lot of scoring. Usually shots of the scoreboard are reserved for time-outs and the end of each period.

4. *Game versus highlight taping.* When you are videotaping a game for a coach to analyze or to obtain player statistics, a wide-angle view is recommended. Try to keep all of the players within the field of view. Keep the camera rolling at all times, stopping only during time-outs or breaks between periods of play. Avoid extreme close-ups, and follow the action on the field of play. Fan reactions, cheerleaders, and other sideline actions are *not* important in this type of videotaping. Follow the suggestions in this chapter for scoreboard and clock shots.

    Highlight videotaping for your school news show, video yearbook, or class reports varies tremendously from complete game videotaping. Some of your best footage will include fan reactions, player "celebrations," and the sights and sounds that accompany the sport. Close-ups and "aesthetic" shots will enhance your videos, as well as some game footage. Your task here is to make the viewer relive these moments and feel the excitement and emotion of the players, fans, and the sport itself.

5. *Reviewing games.* Review parts of each game with the coach or your teacher. Accept suggestions and note areas where taping could be improved. The more games you tape, the more you will improve.

# Dramatic Performances

School plays, musicals, faculty follies, dance recitals, talent shows, and many other school performances are fun to watch but difficult to videotape well with a single-camera system. The problems one often faces include too much or too little light on stage, too large a scene to tape without a lot of panning and zooming, the camera in the way of the audience or the audience in the way of the camera, and of course, the question of "Can I have a copy?" from the participants. Here are some suggestions that can improve your taping skills in this area.

1. *Lighting.* Stage lighting often washes out the faces of the performers. Try using a manual iris setting and avoid the "auto" functions of your camera. Open or close the iris manually as the lighting conditions dictate during the course of the performance. Bring a monitor with you the first few times so you can see how your video looks in color. Viewfinders can be deceiving, especially in low light or extreme lighting conditions. White-balance your camera in the lighting conditions within which you will be taping.

2. *Scene size.* Some scenes are just going to be too large to capture on videotape without standing so far back that everyone will be unrecognizable in the video. Don't worry about videotaping all of the performers all of the time. Follow the action as best you can, staying with the main characters most of the time. *Do not* use a lot of pans and zooms! Occasionally a *slow* zoom and pan of a group will be fine, but do not overuse this technique.

3. *Audience.* Reserve a small area (figure 2.1) to isolate yourself from the audience. Make sure all camera and "mic" cables are securely taped to the floor with masking/gaffer's tape. Place your microphone(s) in an area where they can record stage sound but will not pick up conversations, loud comments and laughs, or thunderous applause from the audience. Sometimes it is necessary to "tape off" a small area for microphones as well as cameras.

## Single-Camera Setups

Place your camera about 9-12 rows back from the stage area. Set up to the left or right of stage center. This location will enable you to obtain close-ups or to cover almost all of the stage action from a wide-angle shot (figure 2.1).

Always use a tripod. Utilize AC power, and bring some extension cords and gaffer's tape.

Sound quality can be improved by placing a shotgun microphone (or two) near the front of the stage on a floor stand and connecting this to your camcorder/VCR. This eliminates the "echo chamber" effect when relying on your internal camera microphone. Use headphones to monitor your sound. If at all possible, record the audio directly from the soundboard into your recording VCR.

Avoid a lot of zooms and pans. Follow the action smoothly and maintain a "good shot" as much as possible.

Follow all copyright laws concerning duplication and sale of videotapes.

Fig. 2.1. Single-camera positions.

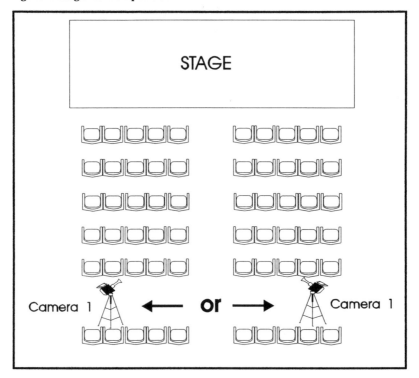

## Multiple-Camera/Switcher Systems

Place one camera 7-10 rows back from the stage for close-ups, and place the other camera far enough back to cover the entire stage scene (figure 2.2).

Sound quality can be balanced and improved by placing one or two shotgun microphones several rows from the stage and using a small audio mixer to balance and mix the sound. Some switchers come equipped with this function.

Avoid a lot of zooms and pans by one camera. Use slow dissolves and cuts to switch camera angles.

Communication between the technical director and the camera operators is important. You can use a wireless or wired headset system. Generally, a wired system will have fewer problems in the long run.

Make sure all cables are taped securely to the floor in any areas the audience and performers are walking over.

Follow all copyright laws concerning duplication and sale of videotapes.

# Miscellaneous Video Production

Within your school are numerous possibilities for creative videos familiarizing students with programs, course offerings, school services, guidance functions and services, as well as many of the school's policies and procedures on a variety of topics. School orientation videos for new students

Fig. 2.2. Multicamera positions.

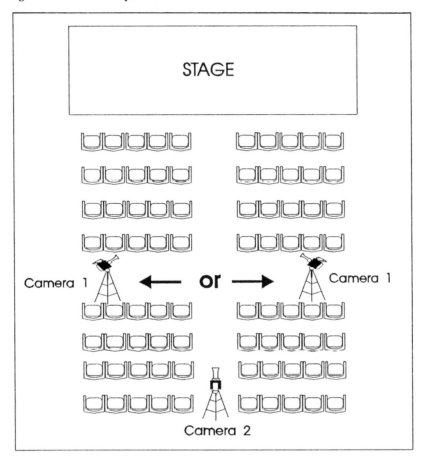

registering at the school, media center orientation videos for classes about to embark on that "research paper" voyage to the library, or teacher education videos demonstrating the latest classroom management practices or discipline strategies are just a few of the topics that may be suggested to you by your principal or teacher during the course of the school year. As you are contemplating production of these projects, here are some guidelines you might find helpful:

1. Have those personnel most familiar with the topic write, or assist in writing, the script. It's hard to research and write about programs and procedures that are unfamiliar to you.

2. Keep the video short and to the point. Only use the essential information. It's an informational video, not an Oscar award-winning movie.

3. Always direct your video to appeal to the viewing audience. A video produced for students should appeal to their likes and interests. Music and dialogue should reflect their norms. Likewise, videos aimed at faculty, staff, or parent groups should also be geared to their interests.

4. Allow plenty of time for planning, storyboarding, and scriptwriting, as well as videotaping and postproduction.

5. Work as a team to complete the job as quickly and effectively as possible. Share ideas and use the talents of all involved. Avoid criticism and encourage everyone to work with a positive attitude.

6. Review your project periodically with your teacher. Revise and review your storyboards as needed. Preview your footage as soon as possible to make sure you have videotaped what you need before you begin postproduction.

7. Always make a backup copy of a tape as soon as possible. Pull out the record tabs on all of your recorded tapes.

Producing school-related videos can be an enriching and rewarding experience for all involved. Establishing guidelines and policies, working closely with your peers as a team, setting appropriate timelines and frameworks, and coordinating production and use of these videos can facilitate and enhance these projects for all involved!

## *Activities: Chapter 2*

1. You have been selected to videotape a Vietnam War veteran speaking to an American history class at your school.

   a. List the equipment you will need to tape this speaker.

   b. What information do you need prior to taping?

   c. Describe some postproduction techniques you might utilize to enhance this video for future use.

2. Plan a visit to observe a science class or laboratory. Discuss possible ideas for videotaping some labs or experiments with the teacher.

   a. What were some tentative ideas suggested?

   b. List the equipment you will need for taping.

   c. What problems do you anticipate might occur, and how will you overcome them?

3. Videotape an athletic event at your school. Shoot 10 minutes of "game" footage, and 5 minutes of "highlight" footage. Preview this footage in class. Identify and compare the differences in style and picture composition, as well as the utilization for the coach and "news show" highlights. Write down your ideas and opinions. Compare them with those of your classmates.

# Equipment Checklist

PROJECT _____ DATE_____

LOCATION _____

_____    video camera(s)/camcorder

_____    VCR

_____    videotape

_____    AC adapter

_____    battery(ies)

_____    tripod(s)

_____    microphone(s)

        _____    lavaliere

        _____    hand-held

        _____    shotgun

        _____    other

_____    lighting instruments _____

_____    monitor

_____    switcher

_____    audio mixer

_____    audiocassette deck

_____    CD player

_____    turntable

# Client Consultation Worksheet

CLIENT: _____     Phone # ( _____ ) _____

PRODUCER: _____     Phone # ( _____ ) _____

Working title:

Target audience:

Suggested program length:

Desired outcomes/objectives:

1.

2.

3.

4.

Resources of client:

1.

2.

3.

Cost of production not to exceed $_____.

Notes:

# INDEX